ONE STEP AT A TIME

ONE
STEP AT A
TIME

A Navy SEAL
Vietnam Combat Veteran's
Journey Home

GREG BURHAM

Including His Hike from Alaska to Mexico

One Step at a Time

www.PhocaPress.com/one-step

Copyright © 2016 by Greg Burham

Cover design by Roman Kuczer

Published by Phoca Press
New York, NY 10025
www.PhocaPress.com

Phoca Press publishes works by, for and about Naval Special Warfare. Our mission is to enhance the public's appreciation and understanding of the contributions of the Naval Special Warfare Community through history up to today.

ISBN-13: 978-0-9909153-4-8

10 9 8 7 6 5 4 3 2

Greg has been fortunate to begin and complete two life changing experiences that most people do not have the opportunity to begin much less complete. His "walk" is one and his military experience in the Navy's UDT and SEAL Teams is the other. Greg was a major part of my military service, as we were in the same UDTB class, UDT-22, SEAL Team TWO and the same SEAL Platoon in Viet Nam. It was an honor to serve with Greg. We had eachother's back through it all and I couldn't have had a better man. No matter how much time has passed, or the distance we have been apart, he will always be my SEAL brother and my true friend.

LT. George A. Ganoung, Class 46E, UDT-22 ST2

I first saw Greg Burham in the spring of 1969. He was in the UDTR class ahead of mine. He was checking out of the Naval Amphibious School while I was checking in. Damn, he was tall! Little did I know at the time that a year later we would be in the same SEAL platoon gearing up for Vietnam. The furnace of combat forges unbreakable bounds of brotherhood between those who experience it together. As I look back through the prism of forty-five years, almost three decades of which was spent on active duty as a SEAL, I remember a time when we were all so young. I was the junior enlisted man in that platoon, also, the youngest and cutest. Eight of the members of SEAL Team TWO Tenth platoon in Vi Thanh retired after long careers as SEALs. Three as Chief Petty Officers, four as Master Chief Petty Officers, and me. There was also a cowboy, a restauranteur, an ATF agent, a photographer, a Boreas Rex (look it up), and a PTSD Counselor. All SEALs form a common brotherhood of warriors, but of those early days I remember two who to this day I call brother whenever we talk or meet; Greg Burham and Keith LeBlanc. Keith was our resident "spook", technically not a SEAL, but in every way one of us. He patrolled with us. We walked the very same trails together. He is every bit my brother as any SEAL who ever wore a trident. I remember sitting on top of a bunker in Vi Thanh consuming copious amounts of Budweiser and Mateus Rose while Keith, Greg, and I solved all the world's problems. So, for Greg, to this very day whither thou goest my friend I am there for you. Except ...maybe not a three thousand mile walk! Wow, what a milestone achievement!

Bob Harger, Commander, USNR-Retired, Class 47-E

The Navy uses a numeric system to evaluate individuals in the performance of their duties. However, the eval, does not address the many personal qualities of the man. As Greg's Platoon Chief, it was my duty to conduct the evals of each man in my Platoon. Of all the evals I had done in my Navy career, the most difficult was, Greg Burham. To mention a few of Greg's qualities..., LOYALTY, in action and word..., SINCERITY, in everything he did..., RESPONSIBILITY, could always be counted on to get the job done..., EXAMPLE, always set a good example for others to follow...., FAIRNESS, absolutely fair and square with others..., COMMON SENSE, to Greg here is no substitute..., PRIDE, took pride in the Navy, the SEAL Team, and did his utmost in developing thesame pride to others..., DETERMINATION, to be the best he could. As you read the book, you will be quick to identify each of the qualities I mentioned. I am proud to have had Greg as a Teammate in SEAL Team TWO and honored to call him MY FRIEND.

Master Chief Bill Bruhmuller, USN Retired

The football arced into the soft blue September sky. The ball glistened in the sun as it flew through pristine Flathead day and settled into Greg's hands deep downfield, running three steps beyond and a head above the pack of junior high defenders. Another touchdown! Years later, I'm standing on first base listening for the crack of Greg's bat. From it's sound I could tell if I needed to run hard to the plate or trot, as the ball cleared the fence, high and deep in left center. What strikes me now is that he never screamed or pumped his fist, or danced in the end zone. There was no "in your face" with Greg Burham. He would circle the bases with a smile and shining eyes. I see now that he was happy for the team. He cared so much for all of us. He always loved the team. I remember the jolt I felt when I heard that Greg had decided to be a SEAL. I knew instantly that he he had the physical and intellectual capability to be a SEAL, but how does a deeply spiritual, gentle soul learn to do what SEALs are called upon to do? How would Greg ever learn to kill? The first time I saw Greg after he came home from 'Nam was downtown in Missoula, Montana. He walked toward me, and he was huge. His strong graceful physique was now packed with muscle. His back was a wedge. He came to work with me at a fitness club I was managing. He was an instant success. The members loved him. Soon the Vietnam scream in his heart began to gain voice. He did his long walk I think so that he could find Leslie, and begin to heal. His scream was shattering. It tried to consume him. It nearly killed him. He laid his soul bare, in public, to anyone who would listen. I believe what saved Greg is love. First of all, the love of Leslie and the kids, and Cela, his Mother. Secondly the love Greg has given to all who knew him came back to him 10 fold. The Creator saved Greg. The moment Arlo and Cela brought young Greg into the world, God looked at him and said, "I need him to serve." God chose him to suffer and survive, and to serve. It has been a pleasure and an inspiration to know Greg Burham for nearly 60 years. I look forward to being his teammate for a few more.

Doug Bitney, Sports Teammate, Colleague, Lifelong Friend

My friendship with Greg Burham was forged over 46 years ago, when we were in BUDS Class 46E at Little Creek, VA. During our time in the teams our friendship grew and remained strong. When we both left the Navy, we took separate paths but always kept in touch. In the mid seventies our paths crossed again. I was attending college in Denver when I accidentally ran into another ex teammate of ours, Bob Kirkwood. Bob was a managing a local trendy restaurant/bar at that time, he gave me a part time job on the spot. Greg had just finished his walk from Alaska to Mexico and was just resting his feet in Montana, so moved to Denver. Greg and I lived together, and the three of us worked at the bar. Greg met his future wife, Leslie, there. They married, moved to Missoula, Montana and started a family, Greg continued with his education eventually obtaining his Masters Degree. He spent his working career with the Veterans Administration as a counselor, and he continues that support of veterans today. Greg's walk through life so far has been an amazing journey, I'm honored to be part of it.For my Warrior Brother and Life Long Friend.

Dick Stauffacher, Class 46E

It has been my good fortune to call Greg a friend and brother over the last nearly half century. We first met in 1970 during the pre-deployment training of our SEAL Platoon to Vietnam. We became what I consider true friends during that deployment and the period of time after our return to the states and my separation from active military duty. Fortunately, within the next couple of years our paths would cross again in Colorado when we would once again "work" together. During the period of time between our military service and our reuniting in Denver, I made a brief entry into the world of business and made subsequent travels, as did many decompressing from a not so popular war experience. During this time, Greg was "traveling" as well. Little did I know, or could I even imagine, that he would spend five months on the "walk" that is the subject of this book. I cannot put into words my sheer astonishment that accompanied Greg's recounting of the yet unnamed One Step at a Time during our time together in Denver. After reflection, I understood that Greg was one of the few individuals that could and would plan, undertake and complete such a monumental goal. Over the years , we have gotten together often and the subject of a book telling Greg's story, which he had documented in a journal and on cassette, would come up. Although it has been some time since his experience and the book getting published, Greg's story is timeless. As you read this book, hopefully you will get to know in some way one of the finest individuals I have had the privilege of being a part of my life. His care for his family, his friends and those depending on him during his career in counseling, especially at the VA, are an inspiration and model to all.

Bob Kirkwood Class 48E UDT-21 ST2

Table of Contents

Dedication

I am eternally grateful for having a very lovable family for my entire life. My dear younger brother Kevin and I were lucky to be born and raised by Arlo Burham and Cela (Jacobson) Burham. Their families of origin also provided us with wonderful grandparents, aunts, uncles, and cousins.

More recently, I am still thankful for being able to meet and marry Leslie Young in Denver during the mid-1970s. She and I then moved back to Missoula, Montana, where we had our own amazing family. Anna and Jon, the twins, were born in 1980, and Jacob in 1984. They continue to make every one of my days worthwhile.

I also respect every combat veteran for risking and, at times, sacrificing their lives, so everyone else can remain safe and free. My main focus is obviously on my UDT-SEAL Teammates. And thank God for the great guys that were in my SEAL Team TWO platoon in Vietnam. If it hadn't been for them, I would not have survived my tour. Hooyah!

Acknowledgements

This book would never have been finished if it wasn't for the help I got from my U.S. Army Vietnam combat veteran partners, Jim Soular and Roman Kuczer.

Jim Soular has edited and expanded the book's text. He is the author of a wonderful book of poetry about Vietnam, *The Thousand Yard Stare*, and is still a writing and literature instructor at Flathead Valley Community College in Kalispell, Montana. Roman Kuczer not only did the cover of the book, but also helped me choose and use several photos and news articles. He is a great graphic artist, now retired.

They are both pictured and mentioned in the "Teach without Teaching" chapter of this book. Roman was one of the Vietnam veterans with whom I went to the Soviet Union with in 1988, and he did the picture of the white and red starred dog tags with their chain shaped like a peace dove. That began as the poster for the Montana Logging and Ballet Company that did a concert to honor us at the University of Montana prior to our trip. We had a great meeting there with the Soviet veterans of Afghanistan to educate and help them with their combat-related PTSD at their request. They appreciated it so much that two groups of them came to the U.S. the following year to visit us. Jim Soular was one of the local veterans who met with them, with Roman and me, here in Missoula, Montana. He was also one of the U.S. Vietnam veteran authors who met with some Vietnamese authors here in Missoula in June 1998 at a gathering organized by the Mike Mansfield Center at the University of Montana.

When I finished my walk from Alaska to Mexico with my UDT-SEAL brother George Ganoung and was staying at his house in Tucson, Arizona with him and his wife Maryleta, I used their cassette tape recorder, my map, and my daily journal, to talk my way back through this hike for eight hours of spoken text. Then I thought that I may want to write a book about my trip someday. It wasn't until 40 years later, in 2014, that Taran Kahler, a computer expert, who is the son of one of my former Missoula Youth Court co-workers, Patta Kahler, helped me convert that eight hours to typewritten text. That became the first phase of this book.

Thank you to Google© for licensing our use of the fantastic maps.

Lastly, I would like to thank Phoca Press and Lisa Merriam for preparing this manuscript for publication.

CHAPTER 1
Why Did You Do This?

I was 25 years old when I began my long walk on June 19, 1974. I suppose it wouldn't be a bad idea to deal with the question that I was asked most frequently during the trip, and that was simply: "Why?"

What possessed me to attempt a walk like this? Normally, if a long, drawn-out explanation seemed a little awkward, I simply attributed the inspiration to stupidity. Everybody chuckled, and some folks even bought it, so I just left it

at that. The longer version, though, goes something like this:

When I was in grade school, I read an article in *Reader's Digest* magazine about a couple guys who rowed a small boat across the Atlantic Ocean, a story that's still pretty vivid. I remember being specifically impressed with the fact that they traveled that far and did it under their own power. I suppose if I can look at any given point in time, this was when I can say the seed was planted for me to take a long trip myself under my own power.

Even as a very young person, doing physical or athletic things made me feel better about myself. I swam, hiked, skied, and rode my bike. I also played baseball, football, and basketball with my dad's help as my coach.

Yours truly when I was three years old.

The Burhams in Kalispell where Kevin, my younger brother, and I grew up with my mother Cela and my dad Arlo.

When I was in grade school, I saw a movie called *The Frogmen* with Richard Widmark, which was about World War II Navy frogmen. Since then, I had always wanted to be a Navy frogman.

My father and all my friends' fathers were World War II veterans and they were honored members of the adult male community because of their military service, which underscored my frogman wish. Growing up in Kalispell, Montana, I loved to snorkel in many western Montana lakes and streams in the summer in between my baseball games.

When I was in high school, all my physical and athletic achievements enhanced my self-worth. Athletically, basketball and baseball were my focus. During the winter, the basketball coaches stopped me from skiing, but I was still hiking, biking, swimming, and snorkeling in the summer during my American Legion baseball season.

Towards the end of high school, I thought about my Navy frogman focus: Do I enter before college as an enlisted guy or graduate first and then go in as an officer? Since I received a basketball scholarship to Spokane Community College in Washington State after high school graduation in 1967, the latter notion of entering as an officer seemed to be my likely path.

Top Row, L-R: Tim Gallagher, Me, Pete Wilke. Bottom Row, L-R: Corky Andrews, Doug Bitney; a few members of my last Legion baseball team.

After my first year at Spokane Community College, during the summer of 1968, I heard that a friend of mine, John Hollow from Helena, Montana, was already a Navy frogman in SEAL Team One! Even though I still had my basketball scholarship for another year, I could not wait. I enlisted in the Navy during the summer of 1968 to fulfill my longtime dream of becoming a frogman myself.

Speaking of physical challenges, I knew that UDTR (Underwater Demolition Team Trainee/Recon) or UDTB (Underwater Demolition Team Basic) training would rank among the greatest physical challenges of my life. That definitely turned out to be the case. Unfortunately, from Navy boot camp in Great Lakes, Illinois, the Navy wouldn't let us go directly to UDTB training, what is today called Basic Underwater Demonlition/SEAL, or BUD/S. I had to wait and to go into training in Little Creek, Virginia after my first duty station

L-R: My cousin Chuck, a former Army Ranger officer, prior to Vietnam with my other cousin Ivan, then my brother Kevin and me.

at Aviation Ordnance "A" School in Jacksonville, Florida in 1969.

Training was six months long, and every single day was extremely physically and mentally challenging! Physically, we would begin the day with a run at 5:30 a.m. and do other extensive exercise sessions: PT (Physical Training), swimming, diving, timed runs on a huge obstacle course, carrying an IBS (Inflatable Boat Small) over our heads and taking long paddling trips with it.

During Hell Week, the fifth week in training, these activities were done 24 hours a day all week long, with only a few minutes sleep interspersed across the days of the entire week.

The sixth week of training was "drown proofing," learning to swim for extended periods of time with our hands tied together behind our backs and our feet lashed together at the ankles.

The trick was to take a deep breath, tuck our chins to our chest, and that would allow our inflated lungs to act as buoyancy and be "above" our non-buoyant heads. We would eventually have to raise our head to exhale and take another breath, and many of us would then sink.

I, along with several others, went unconscious once when I exhaled while I was too far under the surface to grab a quick breath. I went unconscious and started to sink. The instructors let me settle like a falling leaf to the bottom of the deep end of the pool before they jumped in to pull me out. They then pulled me to the side of the pool, still tied up, where I regained consciousness, puking and wheezing for breath.

The instructors didn't ask if I was okay; they asked me if I wanted to quit. I said, "No," and they threw me back into the pool. It only happened to me once, which was enough, but some trainees went through this several times. A key to performing drown proofing correctly was to remain calm. Can you imagine remaining calm after you've just regained consciousness from "drowning?"

At the time I went through training, as long as we didn't quit during drown proofing, we could still move to the next phase of our training. Trainees in that part of SEAL training who didn't make it past drown proofing didn't make it because they made the choice to quit. No one in our class chose to quit during drown proofing week.

There was no way I was going to quit. Consequently, I spent more time in the deep end of the pool until I got drown proofing down. I got through every day by praying I would stay functional. I got to the point—all of us who made it through training got to that same point—where we saw only two options: We would die in training or we would succeed. Quitting was not in the mix. None of us would have ever let the other guys, or ourselves down. Obviously, this was one of the scariest parts of training.

A few trainees were what our instructors called "negatively buoyant," They would sink almost immediately to the bottom. Some would manage to push off the pool bottom and bob to the surface to catch a breath, but a few didn't or couldn't. They, of course, would soon go unconsciousness. We were trained in this manner in case we got injured during combat. Without the use of our arms or legs, we would still be able to float and swim in order to survive. We became "combat swimmers."

Mentally, the instructors would ask all of us to quit several times every day because they wanted us to quit in training, not in future combat. So did everyone else in our class who made it to the Teams.

During a routine check-up (they kept a very close eye on trainees to push us as far as they could without killing us) at Portsmouth Naval Hospital, they ran an EKG on me and discovered an irregularity. The doctor came in to talk to me and I saw the word "DEFECT" written across the top of his report—that nearly stopped my heart. The doctor told me I had a good excuse to quit now. I didn't want to quit! I wanted to be a frogman for as long as I could remember. I begged him to change the report. In the end, he wrote: "NORMAL VARIANT" on it and I was free to continue.

I called my dad every Sunday during training, but the next phase was in Puerto Rico, so I would be out of touch with him for a while. He was so impressed with the training I was getting and told me he was sure I would be a success.

When we had finished training in Puerto Rico, we had a few extra days before we were sent back to Little Creek, Virginia. The Navy put us to good use cleaning the hulls of ships. I was there scraping one morning when one of my instructors called my name. I was afraid I had committed some sort of infraction and dreaded what was next.

After hearing what he said, I would have gladly taken a punishment for any infraction in the world. He didn't have a punishment in mind. He told me that the command had just gotten word that my father had collapsed at work. The instructor had personally arranged for a Red Cross flight to rush me all the way to Spokane where my father as in the hospital.

When I got to Spokane, I got the devastating news. My father had cancer that had spread from his lungs to his brain and stomach.

He was conscious when I got there. I have been told that people hold on and rally when they need to speak to someone. He was defnitely glad to see me and eager to talk to me. My father told me how proud he was of me and how he never worried for a minute that I would quit. He asked me if I was missing training and I told him that we had finished and that the guys would shortly be returning from Puerto Rico to Little Creek for the graduation ceremony. He smiled when I told him all that I was missing was scraping old paint off of ship hulls.

My father lost conciousness shortly after we talked and passed a way about a day later. I remain so grateful to the Red Cross and that instructor for getting me home in time to talk to him.

No one had even known my father was sick. Hewas only 45 years old.

Losing my father, especially just then, was very hard. He was my coach all through childhood and all through training. He was a big force in helping me get through it and it broke my heart he didn't live to see me graduate. Compartmentalizing feelings is something you learn as a SEAL. The loss hit me hard, but life pushed me along fast.

We had a service in Missoula and then I flew back to Little Creek to graduate

Class 46 from 1969 in Little Creek Virginia on Graduation Day.
Front Row (L-R): Billy Acklin, Rick March, Charles Ainsworth, Peter J. Riley and LTJG David Branham.
Back Row (L-R): Ens. George Ganoung, Greg Burham, Rich Smith, Dick Stauffacher and George Shaheen.

with my class. I know my father wanted me to do that.

At graduation, Chief Byers said, "You've graduated and been assigned to a Team, but training isn't over." I now faced a lifetime of training without my lifelong coach, but my father continued to support and motivate me in my heart.

Anyone who thinks you can make it through BUD/S and then sigh in relief is very wrong. We train as hard, if not harder, every single day that we are SEALs. We run. We dive. We jump out of planes. It just never lets up. We never stop being challenged. For me, I was always happiest when putting out my best. I would find out that "training isn't over" would be a theme through my life.

Following that ceremony and after our picture was taken, we were sent to Underwater Swimmer School (SCUBA training) at the Naval Base in Key West,

Florida. That training lasted six weeks. Following swimmer's school, we went to the U.S. Army's Airborne Jump School at Fort Benning, Georgia for three weeks.

Back then, we had Navy SEAL Teams and Underwater Demolition Teams. Members of both were called frogmen. After jump school they sent me to UDT-22. After making it through all that, I felt like I could physically do anything and so did everyone else in our class that made it to the Teams.

On my first cruise with UDT-22, a long deployment to the Mediterranean and back, I remembered that *Reader's Digest* article about the guys who rowed across the ocean. I spent enough time bobbing around on the Atlantic to realize that this wasn't where I wanted to make my trip under my own power. I also realized I wanted to become a different kind of frogman.

After making a couple cruises with UDT-22, I chose to transfer to SEAL Team TWO along with George Ganoung. George was one of the officers with whom I went through training; in fact he was my "swim buddy." A swim buddy is a special concept on the Teams. When you enter training you are assigned to one another and, from then on, we do everything together. Where you go, he goes, and vice versa. You can't be more than a few feet away from one another throughout training. That means we train together, get yelled at together, go to the bathroom together, get punished together. Swim buddies end up forging very strong bonds. When I found out that George and some of my other Teammates from UDT-22 were becoming SEALs, I was surely going with them.

We all began the four months of Vietnam pre-deployment training as soon as we got to the SEALs. We were the 10th Platoon, the last full platoon that SEAL Team TWO sent to Vietnam in late 1970. Thank God I was deployed to combat with those guys!

I know regular Navy or Army guys who were sent to Vietnam by themselves with minimal training. When they

SEAL Team TWO's 10th Platoon in Vietnam (1971)
Front Row (L-R) Pierre Birtz and Joe Hulse.
Second Row (L-R) Dino Pierro, Rodney Pastore, George Ganoung, T.T.,"Ollie" Oliver, Joe "Doc" D'Angelo (on Ollie's shoulder), Bob Harger, and John Engraff.
Back Row (L-R) Greg Burham, Bob Kirkwood, Lowell Gosser, Barry Freece and Chief Bill Bruhmuller.

showed up, they were called FNGs (effing new guys) and shunned for months. The guys already there had seen combat and watched platoon mates die. FNGs were "replacements" for friends who could not be replaced.

We went as a tightly bonded team and we knew we were with people who would never let one another down. We were also fortunate that every one of our senior enlisted guys already had multiple combat tours in Vietnam, and we all went through that training together. It's great to go through pre-deployment training and go to combat with guys who have been through all of that together and who are that focused.

Not letting my Teammates down was the most important thing in the world to me. I was an M60 gunner. During my time in Vietnam, I cleaned my M60 every damned day because when we had rocket and mortar attacks, I was the one on top of a bunker laying down fire if the enemy tried to overrun the base. They didn't for God's sake, but I didn't want to make a mistake. I didn't want my weapon to malfunction. And I didn't want to cause

any of my Teammates to get seriously wounded or killed.

Since most of our seven-month tour was the dry season, our operations were helicopter operations. As the M60 gunner, I was always at the door on the choppers on combat insertions and extractions. I think I got that job because of my size. The M60 is a very large belt-fed machine gun. Not only is it heavy, but it chews through ammunition pretty fast, which itself is heavy. In that job, I was responsible for the safety of everyone on the helicopter.

There was one operation in which one of the Chu-Hoi's came over. Chu-Hoi is Vietnamese for "open arms," which was a program that encouraged North Vietnamese to change sides. Our experience was that Chu-Hoi defectors played both sides, so we had a healthy distrust of them. The operation's focus was on the VCI, the Viet Cong Infrastructure, the guys who were in charge of the VC. VC or Viet Cong, was short for Viet Cong-san, or Vietnamese Communist. They were the Communist Party's own army, distinct from the regular army,

Boat traffic, military and commercial, on the Mekong River in Vietnam.

and active in the North, South and also in neighboring countries.

We were already out on the helo pad and ready to go, locked and

us would have been killed or seriously wounded.

Our tour in Vietnam was seven months. No, I wasn't scared. I was mostly

UH-1C Huey of HAL-3 Seawolves at Binh Thuy, 1970.

A Seawolf, much like the ones we flew into operations across Vietnam. Photo Courtesy the Seawolf Association.

loaded, painted up and everything else, when at the last minute, the operation was canceled. I thought at the time it was probably because of mechanical difficulties with the helicopter. When we got back to our hootch, our living area, we found out that "Bru" Bill Bruhmuller, our Chief-In-Charge with multiple tours in Vietnam, had canceled it.

Bru was involved with questioning this Chu-Hoi. The defector was so insistent that we insert from this direction, this time, this way, that Bru got suspicious. A few weeks later, we learned that the enemy was set up waiting for us, so many of them and so well armed that they probably would have killed all of us and the helicopter crew, as well. Every time I see Bru, I thank him for my still being alive. If he hadn't been suspicious and canceled that operation, many of

concerned about not letting myself or my weapon screw up. If I got killed, or seriously wounded, that would be all right. What I didn't want to have happen is for me to screw up and cause anyone in my platoon to get harmed.

We were set up on a little Army communications base, Vi Thanh, south of Can Tho. I found out through the Phoenix Program, the CIA initiative focused on combatting the Viet Cong, that out of the 44 provinces in South Vietnam, the Chuong Thien Province had more Viet Cong and VC sympathizers than any other province. According to Keith LaBlanc, the CIA operative who worked with our platoon, 75 to 80 percent of all the people there were Communist sympathizers. That's one of the reasons I think they plunked us right in the middle of that province. If we were going to be in the middle of it, we certainly were going to do it right. One of the first things we did when we arrived was build ourselves a makeshift bar in one of the hootches.

When our tour in Vietnam came to an end in early July, we flew home together as a platoon. Not one of us was killed, and for that I remain grateful to this day. I thought back to some of the near misses and thought it was a miracle we were all boarding that plane in the hot humidity of the Viet Nam jungle together. As the tallest guy in the platoon, I was the biggest target. I never get tired of thanking the guys for being there to protect me, not even to this day.

I thought of my father often in Vietnam. The lessons he taught me all through my life served me well there; lessons about teamwork and honor. I think he was a big reason I was able to do my job so well and not be immobilized by fear. Even in the toughest firefights, I kept my cool. I thought to myself, "What is the worst thing that can happen? If I get killed, I will just get to see my father." I did not fear death.

After three quick stops in Japan, Guam and Hawaii, we finally got to the mainland when we stopped at North Island to refuel. I cannot tell you how happy I was to be home. I think I probably kissed the ground I was so happy to be alive and have all of us together.

Vi Thanh, Chuong Thien Province, Republic of Vietnam, February 1971, we are the "men with green faces," ready for an operation in "uniforms" of our own choosing. L-R: Barry Freece, Me, Bob Harger.

I am fortunate to have gone straight to our base in Little Creek, Virginia. SEAL Team TWO received us warmly. No one was spitting on Vietnam vets there. SEALs were greatly admired in Tidewater Virginia, and our brothers on the Teams, many of them also having had their own Vietnam tours, welcomed us.

Bob Harger, one of my Teammates in UDT-22 and SEAL Team Two (we went to Vietnam together with the 10th Platoon), and I rented an apartment in a Chesapeake Bay beach house off the Little Creek Base. It was a perfect set up. Being a SEAL is the greatest thing in the world when you are not getting shot at. Then it was back to training, which I truly loved. I was where I belonged and proud of what we had accomplished together.

I really had no idea what people outside our community thought of the war.

Around that time, a new young officer named Ryan McCombie planned to have about half a dozen of us SEALs make a hike from beginning to end on the Appalachian Trail. The hope was to set a new time record from Maine to Georgia. Ryan got the logistics of this thing planned out and submitted it through the chain of command. As I recall, the Executive Officer and the Commanding Officer of SEAL Team TWO supported it. I thought we were going to be able to do it, but unfortunately someone higher up in the chain of command cancelled it. Another seed for an epic journey was planted, and I was fairly certain that making a long walk was something that I wanted to do at some point. And I was certain that

LT Norris, center, on the radio in "tiger stripe" uniform outside a hootch in Vietnam with his South Vietnamese partner.

25

The smiles, trophies, and the scoreboard all combine to tell the final story in the NavPhib Base Intramural Basketball Tournament as the winning UDT/SEALs line up to receive their honors. Greg Burham (13) won the additional honor of being selected as Most Valuable Player for the tournament. Photo courtesy Rick Smoll.

when I got out of the service, I would be going back out west to Montana.

I felt very lucky that after returning from Vietnam I had another year on active duty with SEAL Team TWO! It was 1971, and many Vietnam veterans were treated like crap by some civilians. Because I was still in the Teams in the Navy, I was insulated from that trauma at first. Spending time and drinking beer with my Teammates made for a very positive post-war experience. Every day we would run, do PT, and, for many months, I attended martial arts classes every morning. That discipline was good for my soul.

We looked out for one another. Even though no one was shooting at us, we still had each other's backs. One of my special Teammates was LT Tom Norris. He was in the UDT Basic Training

Class 45, the class before mine. Our prior Vietnam tours were not together, but we became really close friends in the martial arts class.

That Fall, I wanted to play on the UDT-SEAL football team, but I could not find football cleats at the sporting goods stores big enough to fit my feet, which I complained about to Tommy. Unbeknownst to me, Tommy, after visiting his family in Maryland, returned with a pair of size 13 football cleats for me. If it wasn't for Tommy Norris, I wouldn't have been able to play.

After our martial arts class, Tommy had another tour in Vietnam. During that tour, he rescued two Air Force pilots that were shot down over North Vietnam. In several attempts to rescue the pilots, the Air Force lost a significant number of personnel and aircraft, then abandoned the effort. LT Norris and his South Vietnamese SEAL partner fought their way into North Vietnam and fought their way out to rescue the pilots. For this act of heroism, LT Tommy Norris received the Congressional Medal of Honor.

Back in Virginia, training was not over. We continued to swim, dive, jump out of perfectly good aircraft, and train with weapons and explosives. That fall, I also played on the UDT-SEAL football team, and during the winter, I was on the UDT-SEAL basketball team. They were both great fun. Our football team won many games, and I enjoyed being a wide receiver. Our basketball team won that season's tournament.

Me in fatigues on Little Creek in Virginia Beach just returned from Vietnam.

My enlistment was coming to an end and I began thinking ahead. When I had started college, I thought I would complete my studies and enter the Navy as an officer. Now, with one hitch as an enlisted man, I wanted to complete my education. I had taken two classes at Virginia Wesleyan College nearby, but combining college with the incredible demands of ongoing SEAL training was too much.

The summer of 1972, I left active duty in Little Creek, Virginia after four years in the Navy. Even as I was getting ready to muster out of the service, I still considered staying in and trying to get my degree at night. It was a decision I wrestled with because I loved being a SEAL. Eventually, I decided I would leave the SEALs, return to school, and then possibly return as a SEAL officer. To facilitate that option for me, the executive officer of SEAL Team TWO, LT A. Davis, Jr., wrote a very nice letter of

SEAL TEAM TWO

AMPHIBIOUS FORCE, U.S. ATLANTIC FLEET
U.S. NAVAL AMPHIBIOUS BASE
NORFOLK, VIRGINIA 23521

1 June 1972

From: Commanding Officer, SEAL Team TWO
To: TO WHOM IT MAY CONCERN

Subj: AO2 Gregory Ryan BURHAM, USN, 517-60-7866

1. Petty Officer BURHAM has served with this command for Two years, with his primary duties involving diving, demolition of explosives and parachuting. These are all skills which demand a high degree of maturity, judgement and common sense and Petty Officer BURHAM has amply demonstrated these traits during his assignment here. His conduct and behavior have always been exemplary. Most impressive is Petty Officer BURHAM's dedication and his strong personal desire to improve himself. This attitude is contagious and combined with his cheerful good-natured attitude, makes him a pleasure to be associated with.

2. Petty Officer BURHAM's mental alertness and confident manner are strong indicators of his future success. I would recommend him as a capable individual with great potential to excell in any aspiring endeavor.

3. This command highly recommends that Petty Officer BURHAM, should he decide to do so upon completing his education, be allowed to return to this command.

A. DAVIS, JR., LT, USN
Executive Officer
SEAL Team TWO

recommendation for me that read: "upon completing his education, he be allowed to return to this command."

So I had my plan and started to make my way back to Montana, stopping to connect with as many friends and family as I could along the way. I drove north and spent my first night as a civilian

in Washington, D.C. with a fellow SEAL Bob Kirkwood. He was our Assistant Officer-in-Charge in Vietnam with SEAL Team TWO's 10th Platoon. By then, he was working as a financial advisor in the Washington suburbs.

The next day, I headed west to Washington, Iowa to stay with my Burham relatives Uncle Daryl, Aunt Ella, and cousins Barb and Pat. I loved spending four or five days with them and some of the folks my dad Arlo grew up with. I also got to see Dad's grave for the first time. His older brother Daryl had asked that his body be brought home to be buried in Washington, Iowa where they were born and raised.

My next stop on the way home was St. Paul, Minnesota to see Keith LeBlanc, the CIA officer in Vietnam that we worked with so closely. I had a great time meeting his family, floating down a river on inner tubes, and having beer and barbecue with him. We SEALs lived and operated so

closely with Keith in Vietnam, as he was our Army Intelligence liaison under the auspices of the Phoenix Program, that we considered him one of us. His Vietnamese counterpart was Captain Lu. Keith spoke fluent Vietnamese, and he and Lu interviewed all the guys who used to be part of the regular North Vietnam Army or Viet Cong who claimed they were defecting to our side. The prisoners we took were turned over to Keith and Lu, who would do the interrogation. I was damned glad they had that job, because I didn't want to do any of that stuff.

Even today, every time we have a platoon reunion, we invite Keith. He's told us several times, "Spooks don't have reunions." We consider him one of us because we did so much together and he did such a great job.

Keith LeBlanc in Vietnam.

My aunt Agnes Lorentzen made me this frogman for my birhtday afterI returned fromVietnam in 1971.

As I made my way west to home, I became more and more personally conscious of the anti-Vietnam vet sentiment pervading the country. I had been vaguely aware of it in Little Creek, but that community was very supportive, so I didn't experience much of the mistreatment personally. Coming from a home and family background where veterans were venerated and from a caring community in Virginia, the open disparagement was hard for me to take.

When I got back to Missoula, Montana, I was lucky to live with my mother Cela and brother Kevin. They provided me with a great deal of social support, which I very much needed. People would talk about "crazy Vietnam veterans" in front of me, not realizing I was one. Television shows and movies showed us as cracked and crazed killing machines that were totally warped by the horrors we supposedly inflicted on poor innocent peasants. They were so different from the movies about World War II that honored our heroes. Taken together, the vilification of me and my brothers-in-arms had a very negative spiritual impact on me.

The discrimination was often subtle. If you put on a job application that you were a Vietnam veteran, you could forget about being hired. Even government jobs were hard for Vietnam veterans to get. I felt lucky to be hired as a fitness instructor by Doug Bitney, the manager of Sparta Health Spa. We had grown up together in Kalispell, Montana and played Little League and high school ball together. He knew I wasn't a crazy baby killer and gave me a chance. Doing something physical every day was a form of therapy for me. We joked the reason many Vietnam veterans went to college was that it was easier to get into school on the GI Bill than it was to get a job.

Soon, I enrolled at the University of Montana. My mom was the secretary for the athletic director. She and Emma Lommasson in the registration office were among a few of the University of Montana staff who were supportive of veterans. Most of the staff and the students were strongly anti-veteran.

Back in the early 70s, we didn't tell anyone on campus that we were veterans. I understood the pro-peace, anti-war position, but the anti-military, anti-veteran stuff was very difficult to tolerate. I was standing in line to register and pay my fees when a female student in line behind me saw my GI Bill paperwork. She asked if I had been a soldier in Vietnam. When I said I had gone, she asked me how many kids I had killed and thought it was terrible the government would give a baby killer money for college. I bit my tongue, but the words stung. Of course, it was worse for me. Some guys got drafted and had no choice, but I enlisted, which meant I must have *wanted* to leave Montana to go kill innocent people for no reason other than I was crazy.

Professors blamed the war on us veterans. They said the war was illegal, immoral, insane, and what have you. They talked about American soldiers invading villages to torture peasants, rape women, drop babies from helicopters and burn homes. If you were a veteran, you were either stupid for fighting for "the man," evil or crazy. They made it seem the real patriots were the protesters. The sacrifices I made with my brothers in the Teams were "for nothing." I discovered another Vietnam veteran in one of my classes and we exchanged knowing looks. The only other person you told you were a Vietnam vet was another Vietnam vet. Otherwise, you knew it was best to just shut up.

I didn't date much. When a girl found out I was a veteran, she suddenly was no longer available. She wouldn't answer the phone. I wouldn't see her on campus. In general people let me know what they thought about Vietnam veterans in subtle ways with looks, whispers and gestures.

The negative spiritual impact this had on me was magnified in my church. I was raised and confirmed as a Lutheran in Kalispell. After returning home from the SEAL Teams, I attended a few Lutheran services in Missoula near the University. I never heard the pastor comment about "crazy Vietnam veterans," but some in the congregation would. I would hear stray comments about the crazy, paranoid drug addicts back from Vietnam during the coffee hour after the service. That ended that. I no longer felt welcome in church.

Being raised positively as a Christian, I still felt connected to Christ and was thankful for still being alive. I also thanked my mother, grandmother, and other relatives for praying for me and my Teammates every day. My notion of being a Christian is still "love one another," not "judge one another." When I wanted to feel more connected to God, the Creator, I would walk up into the hills and mountains of western Montana. Nature became my church.

These walks reinforced my notion about taking a long walk someday. After returning to Montana, I loved hiking in the mountains. The when and where of that the long walk I dreamed about, I wasn't sure of, or for that matter how it would be financed. But I did have it in the back of my mind that I definitely wanted to do it. At that point, I was thinking of going from the Canadian border to the Mexican border, so I was hoping to take the Pacific Crest trail.

At the University of Montana, I had read a number of books about folks hiking from Canada to Mexico and Mexico to Canada. But since I was a Team guy, I thought of going one better. We are competitive to the core. I had a cousin building houses in Ketchikan, Alaska, so this Alaskan thing popped into my mind. I did a lot of looking at maps and sat down with a few people and came up with a plan to walk from Alaska to Mexico. Being a Team guy, I knew I could physically do it.

In an article I wrote for a Navy SEAL community magazine called *The Blast*, I explained that leaving the security of the Teams and trying to adjust in a hostile culture was very tough on me. It was about this time that "my emotional wheels started to wobble." I didn't know about Post Traumatic Stress Disorder (PTSD)—it wasn't even recognized as a diagnosis by the medical profession until 1980. I was having symptoms, but couldn't talk to anyone about them. The movies, television and people around town thought Vietnam veterans were crazy and the last thing I wanted to do was tell anything to anyone that would make them think I actually was one of those crazy guys. I tried to pretend nothing was wrong and hoped I wasn't going nuts.

PTSD is not a mental illness, but is a normal response to traumatizing events. Stress following a trauma becomes a "disorder" when left untreated. Events thought to top the list of causes are things like surviving a life-threatening experience, witnessing the serious injury or death of someone (especially someone you care about), or taking a human life. It is easy to see why combat ranks so high among stressful events. Stress tolerance impacts how people react to traumatic events. As men who make it through training to become a SEAL, we demonstrate we have a high tolerance for stress. Operating in teams with the ongoing social and operational support we provide one another raises that threshold to an amazingly high level.

But that is the catch; high tolerance and tremendous support doesn't eliminate the stress altogether. Just because a routine day in the life of an active duty SEAL involves a series of superhuman feats doesn't mean we are no longer human beings. Once we leave the challenging and supportive world of the Teams, we are at high risk of that stress threshold crashing down on us.

As a lifelong counselor in this field, I know all this now. As a young man cut lose and on my own, I was confused, scared and alone. To make things worse, I was telling myself, "stress doesn't bother me. I am a frogman, for God's sake. I thrive on it!" But I wasn't thriving. I tried to gut it out. As a SEAL, I should be able to gut out anything, right?

Ignoring problems doesn't work. In fact, it can make them worse. While still in the Teams, I experienced some nightmares, had a few relationship problems, and had difficulties with anger and drinking. These symptoms got worse and now included a sense of isolation and feelings of rejection. The world thought there was something wrong with me and I feared maybe there was.

The nightmares grew more frequent. I would have flashbacks, too, back to some of the more hair-raising situations we found ourselves in. While in Vietnam we had some really close calls, like getting pelted at night by mortars or landing in a helicopter shot up like Swiss cheese. Coming home, I was so grateful that those close calls always turned out okay. In my nightmares, though, things were different. The close calls went the other way, and my friends were dying in my arms. Somehow it was my fault. In combat, you cannot make mistakes. Your weapon cannot malfunction. I was never concerned about myself. My nightmares were never about me dying, but of me somehow screwing up and one of my brothers paying with his life for my mistake.

I know now as a professional counsellor how important it is to have a safe place to go where people do not judge and where a person can tell their story. So much of what we went through fell into that cliché catgory of "you had to be there." It was hard to explain the chaos, strange situations, horrors, lightning-fast events, and even sometimes, the gallows humor of combat to anyone who hasn't lived it.

The problem is, if you can't find a safe place, you think you deserve whatever happens to you. Having to deal with the self-doubt and confusion all alone, especially back then, when the world was less sympathetic to veterans and we didn't have much understanding of Post Traumatic Stress Disorder, the negativity just builds and builds. It did with me.

When I determined that, indeed, I would walk from Alaska to Mexico, I found my safe place was out there, surrounded by strangers and strange places, where I could find myself. The road was to be my safe place and my story.

Coming back to the question of why I walked, though, I don't think it's all that complex, really. It's kind of an experience thing. Somehow, I guessed I could benefit from an experience like walking from Alaska to Mexico—just like I thought I would benefit from volunteering for the SEAL Teams, from going to Vietnam, or whatever. Some people do things because they feel it'll improve their condition one way or another, and that was the case with this. I felt the experience would be a valuable one, so I figured I'd give it a shot.

It was mid-May of 1974 when I made the final decision, committed myself to the trip, decided to forgo school in the summer, quit my job, and sell my car. It's funny, after making that initial commitment, I never did have any second thoughts about it. It was just one of those things that I felt for one reason or another that I had to do.

Bob Dylan's input:

" How many roads must a man walk down
Before you call him a man?
The answer my friends is blowing in the wind.
The answer is blowing in the wind."

Thank you, Bob!

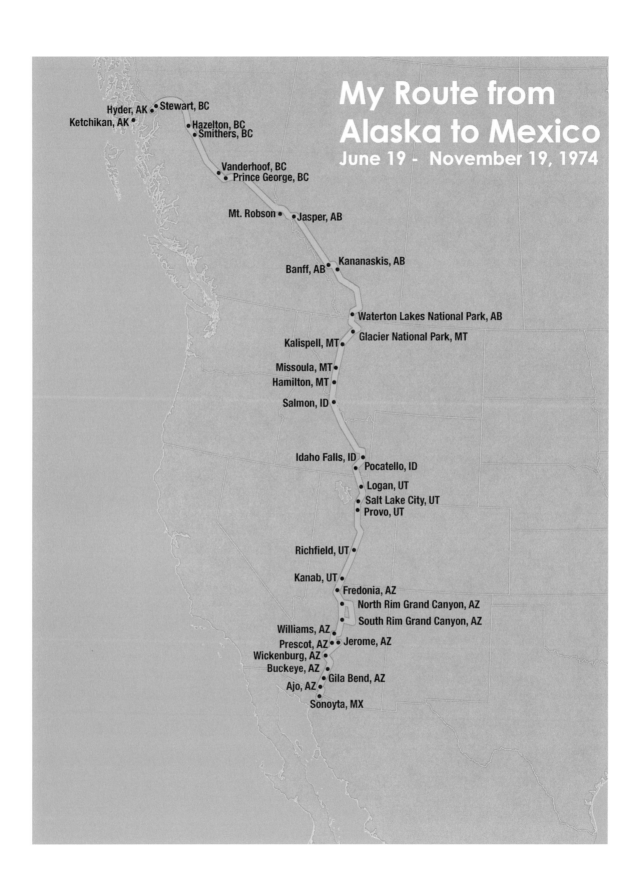

My Route from
Alaska to Mexico
June 19 - November 19, 1974

Hyder, AK
Stewart, BC
Ketchikan, AK
Hazelton, BC
Smithers, BC
Vanderhoof, BC
Prince George, BC
Mt. Robson
Jasper, AB
Kananaskis, AB
Banff, AB
Waterton Lakes National Park, AB
Glacier National Park, MT
Kalispell, MT
Missoula, MT
Hamilton, MT
Salmon, ID
Idaho Falls, ID
Pocatello, ID
Logan, UT
Salt Lake City, UT
Provo, UT
Richfield, UT
Kanab, UT
Fredonia, AZ
North Rim Grand Canyon, AZ
South Rim Grand Canyon, AZ
Williams, AZ
Prescot, AZ
Jerome, AZ
Wickenburg, AZ
Buckeye, AZ
Gila Bend, AZ
Ajo, AZ
Sonoyta, MX

CHAPTER 2
Taking Off and Heading to Alaska

I fully intended on making the trip a year later in 1975, spending the interim saving for it and getting everything ready. But things aligned themselves such that it was either this year, or I had a feeling that I wouldn't make the trip at all. In order to finance it, I had to sell my car and a few things that I had that were worth something and get enough money together to support myself for the time it would take. I planned to take a year off. I'm kind of glad that I didn't take that long because I don't think I would have had the money to support myself for that whole year.

I planned a route that would take my walk from Hyder, Alaska, through Missoula, Montana, so I could be the best man at my younger brother Kevin's wedding later in the summer. I would have to move fast to make that schedule.

The people in Missoula, both friends and family, were tremendously supportive. Their encouragement made me feel better already. It felt good to have a challenge in front of me. Instead of the guy trying to fit in, I was the guy going on an adventure. That is a core part of being a SEAL, and it turns out a core part of who I really am. Getting ready for the trip, training physically, and mentally setting my goals, made me feel like me again, not the "Crazy Vietnam Vet."

My Teammates, my friends and family did whatever they could to help

me get ready for the trip. And that took some doing, because I had, at that time, less than a month to go before I was to take off. I knew that the longer I waited in to June, ultimately the worse the weather would be down the line. So it was kind of a frantic time there for a few weeks, getting everything sewed up and ready to go. I suppose that without the extra help, I wouldn't have been ready in time.

Two of my cousins from Kalispell, Montana, Chuck and Ivan Lorentzen (our Norwegian mothers were sisters), both had extremely important roles in the beginning of my walk. Ivan volunteered to drive me to Seattle, Washington to catch the Alaska Marine Highway Ferry and take it up to Alaska. His older brother Chuck was a structural engineer building houses in Ketchikan, Alaska, the destination for the ferry. I also planned to stay with Chuck for a couple days. Fortunately, that wasn't very far from Hyder, Alaska, where I was going to begin my hike.

The night before Ivan was going to pick me up in June, I went out to have a beer. One of my Missoula friends was there and showed a little more than an average interest in the trip because he had never been to Alaska before. He was a guy by the name of Buzz Blastic. He always told people it was "plastic" with a "B." He was a hiker, an outdoorsman and a skier. He was a married high-school teacher in Missoula.

As we talked, his interest in the trip grew. He didn't want to walk all the way to Mexico, but he did want to see Alaska. Right there in the bar, he talked to Beth, his wife. She knew he really wanted to go, so she agreed to let him do that. He figured he'd be gone for two weeks. So there it was decided, just like that. He really wanted to start the trip with me, which added to my enthusiasm. I had always thought I would do this trip alone, but it felt good to have a "swim buddy" for the start of it and it felt good that so many people were so supportive and so excited for me. It was a feeling I hadn't had for a very long time; certainly not since I returned from Vietnam. Buzz was a really fine, fine person. I was glad for him and for me that Beth strongly endorsed his starting the trip with me, and I was grateful for his company.

The next morning, my journey began. Ivan came down from Kalispell and the three of us set off for Seattle. I started keeping a daily journal as we left Missoula. We had a great trip with beautiful, sunny weather. We drove the first day to Spokane, and we stayed with a couple good friends of mine, Pete and Beth Wilke. Thank you, Pete and Beth! Pete and I had played baseball together in Kalispell. We spent the following afternoon at the Expo '74, the first environmentally themed world's fair. We all had a good time there. I hadn't been back to Spokane since I stopped attending junior college before enlisting in the Navy. We were all impressed with how they had renovated the river portion of the city for the Expo. It really looked beautiful.

Buzz said he had to have a traveling hat. We went all over town looking for one for him. I had already bought my Stetson in Missoula. In the window at this western outfitter store in Spokane was a huge Tom Mix Stetson. Buzz said he had to have that. Someone called it a "Ten-Gallon Grey Stetson," and he got it. The thing was just huge and really neat. After that, we jumped in the car and continued the trip to Seattle across the flat land in central Washington.

When we arrived in Seattle, Ivan took us to REI (Recreational Equipment Incorporated), so I could get the rest of the equipment I needed for the trip. Since Ivan's older brother Chuck was a house builder and a structural engineer and

Packed up, loaded up and ready to begin.

had worked in Seattle before moving to Alaska, we wound up staying in a house that he and a friend had built, but had yet to sell. It was a brand new house, but wasn't quite finished yet, so the three of us were camping in sleeping bags in this great house. It was a neat night.

The next morning, Ivan drove Buzz and me to catch the ferry. Thank you very much, Ivan! The Alaska Marine Highway System has a ferry that runs north from Seattle. It stops in Prince Rupert, British Columbia first and then in Ketchikan, Alaska, where Buzz and I got off. The ferry ride to Ketchikan was a fantastic, two-day journey. It's a beautiful, beautiful trip. If you ever get a chance to take it, do. It's along the inland waterway where it's green, unpopulated, and wonderfully scenic.

It's kind of interesting to explain accurately my feelings as the ferry pulled away from the pier in Seattle.

Leaving the lights of Seattle behind was kind of like severing a lot of ties and being overwhelmed by a new sense of freedom. We were going to a place that Buzz and I had never been before and always wanted to: Alaska. It was a very free feeling.

In order to better understand this freedom thing, know that it is related to the time when I got back to Montana after the military and saw a lot of the people whom I cared for very much. Many of the guys I had gone to high school and junior college with, because of athletic injuries or one thing or another, hadn't had to go into the military. As a consequence, I had the feeling that I was four years behind everybody because they all had college degrees and their own businesses, and some already had wives and families. I realize now that it may sound ridiculous,

but I had the idea that I had to catch up with them, with what they were doing or what they were into.

I enrolled at the University of Montana as a first step in catching up. I was going to school on a full-time basis and was lucky to get a full-time job. I was doing both things fulltime, year around. It was through the summer, too, to make up for "lost" time, up until the time I left on the trip. My time really wasn't my own for the two years that I spent out of the service. I was very fortunate to have family, friends, and a job that I loved in Missoula, but being treated like an "Evil/Crazy Vietnam Veteran" at the University of Montana was difficult. So was watching so many TV programs and movies that had the perpetrators and villains be Vietnam veterans. The stress just kept building.

When I told people I was going to walk from Alaska to Mexico, some of them said I was crazy, but it was an entirely different kind of crazy. I was free from the day-to-day grind of school and work. I was free from being judged negatively. I had nothing before me but the open road and the incredible beauty of nature. This gives you some idea of why this freedom thing was such a big deal for me. From all kinds of pressure to none at all felt great.

The weather was perfect, the sun was shining, and the people on the boat were very nice. Buzz, of course, was there the whole time. He is a fantastic individual; the kind of guy who's "up" all the time. He's comical and talented. You can't help being "up," too, when you are with Buzz. What a perfect companion for starting the adventure.

There was a cocktail lounge on the ferry, and one night Buzz and I and some people we had met on the boat went in and had a few drinks. One guy showed up with a guitar. It was really nice because Buzz played the guitar, and between those two guys and the rest of us, we did a poor job at singing, but we had a very fun time. The whole bar was singing the "Folsom Prison Blues," and you name it. Buzz is just that kind of a guy. He is always in the middle of everything and is always making people laugh and enjoy themselves.

When he and I arrived in Ketchikan, Ivan's older brother, my cousin Chuck, met us at the ferry and showed us Ketchikan. Ketchikan is on a side of a rock on an island. Chuck said they get about 150 inches of rain a year, and it never gets extremely cold, because it's pretty far south on the panhandle. Because of its rocky island nature, half of Ketchikan is on pillars out in the bay. It looks like the town was built temporarily, yet it's been there a hundred years. Walking around town is fascinating because a lot of the streets are just sidewalk steps running up and down hills. One of the streets is largely on these pillars over the bay. Chuck was telling us about one drunk who drove off the higher road and fell right downhill, crashing through the roof of a bar on the street below. That might have been more than

a little startling. There is a banner across the main street in Ketchikan proclaiming that it's Alaska's third-largest city. That's compelling, because I can't imagine that the population was over 10,000 to 15,000 people.

Alaska is really quite a place. You expect all the people there to have a pioneer spirit because the entire state is a frontier. It's mostly people who have just decided for one reason or another to pick up everything and try something new. It's really a neat place, but the prices are a bit higher than the Lower 48. I expect that it has to do with the supply channels. Of course, everything has to be flown or boated in, thus the expensive prices. Buzz and I were out seeing the town one day and stopped for just a cheeseburger and cup of tea, and it did cost more twice than it would have in Montana.

We stayed with Chuck for three or four days, I believe. We got to meet some of his friends, too. One was a lady by the name of Juanita, who owned a great restaurant in Ketchikan. I would like some day to return and see a few of those folks.

CHAPTER 3
Beginning the Hike

It was on a Wednesday morning, June 19, that Chuck took Buzz and me down to the pier in Ketchikan where we hopped on a float plane mail flight and flew to Hyder, Alaska. It was really a breathtaking trip. Thank you very much for helping us get started, Chuck! Most of that portion of Alaska and British Columbia is muskeg, which is what they call a swamp up there, so it's largely uninhabited. We saw a moose plowing through all the muskeg, and the ground, which was vegetation floating on the water, just kind of waved away from him. Buzz had never flown in a small, fixed-wing aircraft, so he was totally awed, by not only the scenery, but also by the ride itself.

Buzz and I at the start of the trip in Ketchikan — with Buzz in his impossibly large hat.

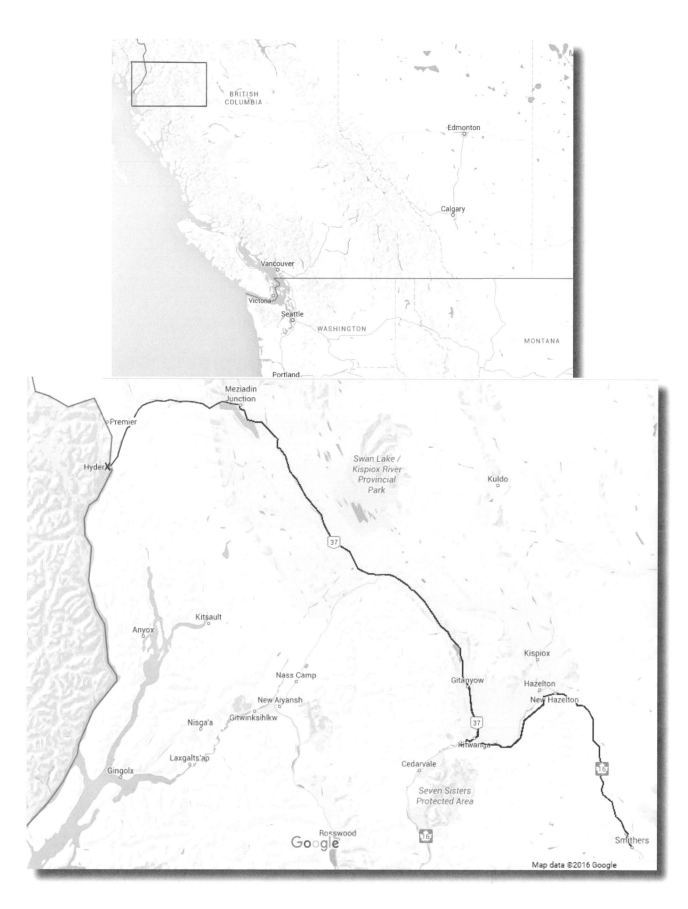

We set down in the bay in Hyder and walked from the pier to a little restaurant and had breakfast there. Hyder itself is billed as Alaska's friendliest ghost town. There were 40 people living there at the time. It's kind of backed up against a glacier and surrounded by the rest of British Columbia. The folks there said that at one time there were about 4,000 people in Hyder when the gold mines were active.

My spirits were awfully high as we strode out of town. There was a little customs booth at the Canadian border, but no one was in it. I believe the reason for that was because there isn't much traffic for the Border Patrol to manage between those two small towns. Stewart, British Columbia, was only two miles from Hyder. As a result, my notion has always been that Buzz and I literally started with "one foot in Alaska." When we got to Stewart, we stopped in this little place and had a beer to celebrate the fact that "The Hike" had officially begun!

It was kind of a grey day, so we spent a little time in town. We wrote a couple of post cards, had lunch, and then

Buzz and I in Ketchikan in front of the float plane that would take us to Hyder.

took off. The sign as we left Stewart said New Hazelton was 170 miles away. At that time, 170 miles really didn't register with me. I was still thinking of driving 170 miles, not walking, so it didn't strike me; 170 miles seemed no big deal.

That day we only made about 12 or 13 miles and then camped in my great two-man tent by a river. The river was low, down a bit from where it had been during spring runoff, so we pitched my tent in the sand and hoisted our packs up into the trees because there were a lot of signs of bears in the area. We talked to a few people in Stewart, and they said that they had seen several grizzlies and other kinds of bears quite frequently in the area.

We were in the process of making camp, hoisting the packs up, and cooking dinner when we ran across a bear track that was startling—it was so damn big.

It was in the sand and looked like it had been made some time ago, but it still made us a little tense. We also saw where he or she had spent the evenings and where it had scratched a tree to sharpen its claws about 9 or 10 feet up. Obviously, we sure didn't want to run into that one.

It was lightly raining that night and was still raining in the morning when we got up. As we packed the tent, it was wet with a lot of sand in it. We had breakfast underneath a nearby bridge to get out of the rain for a little while and get everything packed up.

We were both a bit physically challenged, even from our first short day. The packs were heavier than they should have been, I guess. Our notion was that if we had a lot of things that we really didn't need, it would be better to have them and be able to throw them away, rather than

Buzz taking in the breathtaking scenery as on the road out of Stewart.

not to have the things we needed once we were in the wilderness.

The river we stayed by and got our water from was running pretty fast and was still a bit silty, but that didn't matter much because we were staying pretty thirsty. We used our filters and drank it any way. We enjoyed breakfast, put our rain gear on, and took off.

The rain persisted throughout the day, but we were glad it was knocking down the mosquitoes and black flies. It would hold up for a little while and then start again. It was fun to watch Buzz as he skipped down the road in the rain with that big hat.

The dirt road we were on wound around a mountain and started to wend its way through a pass. Up on the pass were some of the most phenomenal waterfalls I have ever seen in my life. They were glacier-fed, and every once in a while, we would catch a glimpse of the glacier over the mountain tops. I'm not certain of the exact elevation of these mountains, but because we were at or near sea level, it probably did make them seem a lot higher than they were. This coastal range in this area gets quite a bit of rain during that time of year, so everything was very, very green. The walk was truly beautiful.

It was day two of the trip, so we were both prone to frequent breaks. We'd stop, sit down and catch our breath for a while on a regular basis. Our packs were a bit heavy, especially loaded with sand. Buzz had a little more sense than I did because he hadn't brought quite as much stuff as me.

My discomfort focus at this point was my shoulders and hips with the heavy pack. My legs were fine. To prepare for this trip, I had been doing quite a bit of weight training and distance running to strengthen my calves and thighs. I didn't give my shoulders and hips quite enough of a workout and I was sore.

Before the rain stopped, we happened upon a road construction outfit. Their big trucks went by us frequently. The rain that we didn't get coming down, we got in our faces coming up from the muddy dirt road as the trucks churned by. Our spirits remained high nonetheless. Late one afternoon, the rain let up, and it was really pretty. A rainbow in a northern rainforest is very impressive.

Late that afternoon, as we were trying to find a place to camp, we came upon a snow field. It was at the foot of one of the glaciers that came right down to the road. We were scouting the place out,

One of the glaciers we encountered in Bear Glacier Provincial Park.

and while we were there, the glacier was cracking and rumbling as sections of it broke off. We decided it might be safer—and more restful—to move a distance down the road. We took a picture, then ended up camping about a half mile down from the glacier.

The night of June 20 was spent by a little creek not far from the road. Because we were so far north in June, the nights were short. Even sleeping in daylight, it was very restful because we were both pretty tired. During the early days of the hike, I was still making campfires every night to make the nights more comfortable. As time progressed, I found I didn't need to do that. I soon didn't bother with things like campfires to heat my water or food. As a SEAL, I really didn't need little comforts like that.

In the early summer days of the start of our hike, the sun would go down, and the land would finally get dark around 11 or 11:30 p.m. Around 4:00 a.m. or so, the sun would be up again. Initially, it was a little hard to get used to sleeping when it was light like that, but we both so tired every night that it didn't take long to become accustomed to it.

The next day was extremely beautiful. The sun was shining, and we were right by this little stream. We ate breakfast, which usually consisted of granola or oatmeal, powdered milk, raisins, and nuts. We had a good supply of food and consistently ate pretty well. Most of our lunch and dinner meals would consist of rice or dried goods of some sort, and we had a load of freeze-dried meals, too. We used a little mountain stove for heating the water and cooking our freeze-dried food.

We didn't get started until around noon. A few miles from where we

A glacier snakes between two mountains.

44

started, the road forked, and the lower road was blocked off. We took the high detour and climbed up on this little hill. It took us to a point high above the foot of the aforementioned glacier. It was unbelievably beautiful and so blue it almost looked animated. The sun was shining on this glacier as it snaked right down to the road below us and formed a little lake where it had been melting. Parts of it had broken off and were floating there. It was really funny to see scenery that spectacular and not have a load of other people around enjoying it, too.

That was another thing that really impressed me about this country: It was beautiful and there were so few people up there. The little dirt road wasn't traveled very frequently, and some of the scenery was phenomenal. The clouds of mosquitoes and black flies that continued to plague us might have had something to do with that. We used the insect repellant in generous amounts, but it didn't seem to do much.

On the downside of the hill, we stopped for a little break, had some jerky, and slapped a few mosquitos. I noticed the soles of my boots were parting a little bit. I mentioned it to Buzz, and he smiled, not too concerned. They didn't look too bad, and I hoped they would hang together to Hazelton or a place where I could either get them fixed or buy another pair.

Our destination for June 21 was a place with a little lake. We hoped to camp by that lake, and Buzz, being an avid fisherman, was really looking forward to seeing what he could catch. We got there around 9:00 at night, but it wasn't dark yet. The road passed by the lake, but it didn't go down to it. We were keeping our eyes out for a way to get to the shore. We came across a stream that went under

A beautiful glacier-fed lake.

the road and looked as though it made a pretty good trail to the lake, so we started following that. Quite rapidly, the rain forest closed in around us. We kept trying to blaze a trail. Buzz went first, and I followed him. The vegetation was so unbelievably thick that we thrashed, tripped, and cussed all the way down to what we hoped was the beach. No such luck. It was a sheer rock drop-off. Unfortunately, eggheads that we were, our jaunt was conducted in walking shorts. Since there wasn't a beach, we turned around and thrashed our way back toward the road. We had to laugh at ourselves because we were just covered with scratches and welts.

After resting a little while and getting ourselves back together, we saddled up and shuffled down the road, only to find a path to the lake less than a quarter mile away. We found a great place to camp and bought a six-pack of beer from some local campers. Our banged-up condition and the wonderful setting influenced our decision to stay an extra day through Saturday, June 22.

Fishing and relaxing with the help of that stout Canadian beer helped us sleep extremely well both evenings.

The first morning, as Buzz was fishing and I was trying to get up enough nerve to take a bath in the glacier-fed lake, a young Canadian man came up to us and introduced himself. He was Eric McDonald, a seasonal worker for the British Columbia Highway Department. Eric helped me lighten my pack by buying my bow and arrows with accessories. Eric took us up to the highway camp, and we both had a shower and a really good home-cooked meal. We had only been out a few days, but the rain and the mosquitoes made it seem like a lot longer.

The highway camp was utter luxury to us.

The next morning we had breakfast, packed up and said goodbye to Eric and the people at the highway camp who had been so nice to us and headed out. It was kind of a grey morning, but it was cool and it wasn't raining, which made it nice for walking. That day we were able to knock out 15 or 20 miles. Most of our way was through bottomland as we moved away from the coastal range. The mosquitoes and the black flies were unbelievable, buzzing us and giving us painful bites. Repellant had no impact. When we stopped for lunch, it looked like lord of the flies. These things were just bathed in insect repellant, and still they were hovering about a foot away from our heads and dropping into our food. I heard stories while in northern British Columbia about hordes of mosquitos ascending on mule trains and driving the stock insane. There is no doubt in my mind that those stories are completely factual.

When Buzz and I hit the road again, he talked of hitchhiking to Jasper. I can't say that I blame him. The bugs were bad. We were not making very good time. He wanted to see other things in Alberta before he went home. He had never intended to make the whole walk with me, so I didn't feel disappointed. We talked it over, and he determined he would be leaving the next morning.

After breakfast, we spent about half an hour shuffling gear back and forth. I gave Buzz a lot of the things I didn't think I'd need then so he could take them back to Montana for me. We got all this shuffled around and packed up and repacked. The separation of my boot soles was worse, so we tapped them together with some duct tape and headed out. About a half an hour down the road, a white Volkswagen Bug pulled over and asked if we wanted a ride. Buzz took it. I don't think I will ever forget seeing that white Bug go down the road and carrying him around the corner.

Having a "swim buddy," especially Buzz, made the start of my hike special. I appreciated having someone to help me acclimate and to enjoy the beauty of the road with me. Still, this was always a walk I needed to make alone. That was a big part of the challenge and a big part of the journey of discovery. I lightened my pack in those early days and also began to lighten my emotional baggage. We had walked a little more than 100 miles together. The hike was now mine. There was a lot of country out there, and it felt like that was all mine, too.

The remainder of that day was pretty uneventful. The road was lined with lodge pole pine and birch. It was just a matter of walking it out; it was a relatively monotonous stretch. I stopped asking touring motorists about distances. Nobody riding in a car was really keeping very close track of mileage. Part of being a SEAL is doing whatever it takes, for as long as it takes, for as far as it goes. I was walking the distance, whether ten miles or twenty, so it didn't really matter.

Motorists passing in the opposite direction kept telling me about a lake that was supposedly just a couple more miles down the road, but wound up to be closer to nine. Thank goodness I finally made it to the little lake, and it was a very beautiful spot, every bit worth the journey. I was exhausted when I arrived, but it was a very tranquil setting. The lake was like a mirror with snow-capped peaks from the coastal range in the background. Unfortunately, millions of mosquitos made it there before I did. I set up camp, made a fire, and was grateful that the smoke kept a few of them away. My dinner was a freeze-dried meal, and after that I turned in. That evening I noticed that my toes were becoming blistered on top because the tape holding my boot to the soles was pushing down across the top of my foot, creating a hot spot. The good news was that it wasn't any big deal so far.

The following morning brought sunshine. I packed up, had breakfast, and was off. Unfortunately, the tape on the toe continued to pinch the boot down to aggravate those blisters. Because the tape was holding the boot itself together, there wasn't too much I could do about it, but just tolerate it and keep walking. During the next few days, I was frequently reminded of what Chief Byers, our senior instructor in UDT training, would often say: "Training is not over." In SEAL training, you quickly learn that pain is just pain and it won't kill you. You train to accept discomfort as a regular part of living, like breathing.

I finally came to a junction in the dirt road and headed south for Hazelton. Over five days of walking and I had not yet hit the first major town. 170 miles is really 170 miles when walking through rain and mosquitos with worsening blisters.

Many folks continued to stop and ask if I needed a ride. One of the women asked me if my wife or girlfriend was missing me. I just said, "No, I'm not married," but didn't explain to her that all the young women I dated before, during, and after the military were not treated very well by me, so I wasn't missed by them. The only woman who did miss me was my mother.

I would go on and thank them all for making their offers and explain to them that I was walking to Jasper, Alberta, and they found that very hard to believe. That was why I couldn't imagine letting them know that I was really headed for Mexico. I didn't want anyone to think I was crazy. I could have stayed home in Montana for that.

I also didn't tell anyone that I was a Vietnam vet for the same reason. This walk was the beginning of a new story for me, one where I wouldn't have to endure angry looks, mumbled insults or take responsibility for geo-political dynamics over which I had no control. I had no idea what the average Canadian thought about the war and didn't want to find out. To them, I was just a hiker and that was fine with me. Hiking and enjoying nature was perfectly acceptable. So people might think I was foolish to turn down a ride, but I felt better being thought of as stupid than crazy.

Most of the folks who stopped to offer me a ride and who took the time to chat for a while were really nice. Some of them would shake their heads when they heard what I was doing, and some would even call me crazy. One week down the road, the word "crazy" no longer meant "nuts." People used the word crazy to say that what I was doing was admirable, ambitious, inspiring, even a little heroic. I was doing something that earned respect, not jeers. All my life, I always felt good about myself through physical exertion and through pursuing goals. Now nearly every minute of my day was fill with both. My emotional wheels, wobbling back home, were running truer and truer with each mile I walked.

One elderly couple gave me a root beer, and one younger couple came by and gave me a can of 7-Up. One younger guy stopped, and he and his girlfriend chatted with me for quite a while. As he was leaving, he gave me a Budweiser. Those things nourished my soul.

My body, however, wasn't faring so well. That evening I pitched my tent, and after I finished dinner, I checked out my feet. The blisters were getting a bit worse. For some reason, my right foot wasn't quite as bad as my left. There was no one to complain to and nothing to be done. All I could do was start to worry.

There was quite a bit of logging activity along this dirt road. That gave me the opportunity to set my tent up in the tracks of their heavy equipment, which gave me a little shelter, with softer, more level ground. Because the loggers were cutting a lot of the trees down by the side of the road, the open space allowed the wind to blow harder. The good news with that was that the breeze was blowing many of the bugs away, so I was needing much less insect repellant.

That night I cleaned and put new bandages on my feet and decided to begin walking the next day in my leather track shoes, not those damn boots. Since the boots were worthless and heavy, I just threw them away by the side of the road—after taking a picture of them.

From that day forward, my feet did much better in my track shoes. The iodine tincture that I was using on my blisters helped a bit, but not too much. I realized I was in trouble. My feet wouldn't stop swelling and were now bleeding. Worse, the glands in my groin had begun to swell, as well, meaning I had an infection that had spread beyond the blisters. I had no choice but to take the next ride I

My taped boots.

was offered the following morning. I was hoping that in New Hazelton I could find a new pair of boots and get some medical help for my blisters. When a logging truck pulled over, I jumped in.

It was strange to cover a day's hike in ten minutes. The kind logger who gave me the 15 mile ride dropped me off in New Hazelton near the Totem Pole Café. I was very glad to be able to have the first good meal I had had in quite some time. As I entered the café, I left my big pack inside the door and noticed some very unusual glances cast my way. When I got to the men's restroom, I looked into the mirror and saw why some folks were looking at me like that. Wow! Was I ever a mess! My hair was matted down and dirty, my clothes were dusty, and my beard was half grown and a mess, too. I looked scary crazy.

After recovering from my own shock, I cleaned up a bit before going back into the restaurant. Thank God, I was able to order an amazing breakfast! I ended up eating two entire breakfast meals and topped them off with a hot fudge sundae.

After that, I went outside and discovered that New Hazelton was such a small town that I couldn't find a boot store or a drug store. Since I was now off the dirt road and onto Yellowhead-16, the Trans-Canada Highway, I began to walk towards the larger town of Smithers, British Columbia. Late that afternoon, someone offered me a ride and took me there.

Smithers is a great town with a population back then of about 4,200 people with an elevation of about 1,600 feet. It's nestled at the bottom of the Hudson Bay Mountains in a green valley called the Bulkley Valley. It's a very picturesque spot.

I was determined not to let a potential systemic infection stop me from walking every last step from Alaska to Mexico. I figured that the rides that I took amounted to somewhere between 40 and 60 miles. So I decided that when my feet were healed up and I got my boot situation straightened out, I'd hitchhike back north of Hazelton to the spot where I took the first ride and make up the distance I had ridden on foot.

Later that afternoon, I checked into the least expensive hotel I could find in Smithers, which was the Smithers Hotel downtown. It was a great place. After more than a week in the cold, rainy, bug-infested mountains, I felt that I was staying at Caesar's Palace. After I checked in, I took a shower and cleaned up. I must have lost at least 10 pounds of grime in the

shower. I had a great night's sleep, and the next morning I grabbed the cleanest dirty shirt I could find, re-bandaged my feet, and struck out to see if I could find some boots. Unfortunately, that wound up to be a dead end. There were some nice sporting goods stores in town, and some did have hiking boots, but none of them had any big enough for me.

Later on that afternoon, I called home and talked to Mom and my younger brother Kevin for a while. It sure was good to hear their voices. My main reason for calling was to ask Mom if she'd mail me my other pair of hiking boots. They were only about half broken in, but at least they fit very well.

Smithers turned out to be a real friendly little place, and I'm glad because I had to spend some time there waiting for my feet to heal and for my boots to

Panoramic view of the Smithers Valley looking at the Babine Mountain Range.

get there. I continued to shop around town for a while and was amazed that I couldn't even find a pair of socks that were big enough for me.

Later on that afternoon, I met a druggist in a local pharmacy by the name of Pat. He recommended some antibiotic ointment for my feet and an oral medication for the infection that had spread. The stuff I got from him started to help my feet look and feel better. Thanks, Pat!

My next night at the Smithers Hotel was not as restful as my first. I was clean and well-rested, so perhaps I was just now noticing the flaws in my hotel selection. My room was directly above the hotel bar, and at about 8:30 that night, the music started. Not too long after that, a couple of the folks that had been in the bar were confronting each other on the sidewalk. I don't know if they ended up fighting, but they continued to make noise into the evening. Sadly, I didn't get as much sleep that night as I did the night before. I got up fairly early the next morning and checked out of that false Caesar's Palace.

I had a good breakfast, and because my feet were feeling better I got back on the road at about 9:00 that morning. I thought that I could get an early ride to Hazelton or a little beyond that, so I could start walking back over the areas where I accepted rides. I had no such luck. Nobody even slowed down to pick me up. Since my hitchhiking didn't work, I decided to just walk on the other side of the highway and make up the distance. I was meticulous about not cheating it one single footstep.

My tent and campsite in Smithers.

While I was doing that, I encountered a couple of guys who were riding bikes in the other direction. They were from California and had biked up to Seattle to take the same ferry Buzz and I did to Prince Rupert, and were now headed for Jasper, Alberta. It was nice to talk to somebody from the States.

A Wyoming car blew by me that afternoon. I waved at them, but they didn't wave back. Because I was such an odd-looking dude, that didn't surprise me at all. A man with a bit of a British accent stopped later on that day and said he had done some what he called "touring," himself and offered me a bit of encouragement. That ended up being very helpful! Emotional support meant more to me than the best boots in the world.

I ended up just walking about 30 miles northwest of Smithers that day and camped by the highway. I spent that evening by the Bulkley River and had a very peaceful, restful, enjoyable evening. The next day, I just hiked back to Smithers. With those miles, I had made up for the rides I had taken, and then some.

Obviously, I was still walking in my track shoes, and my feet were healing nicely. Walking that couple days was awfully nice. I had some rain and some sun during both days and met some truly nice people. Some of the other good news was that bugs in the Bulkley Valley were evidentially banned. They didn't give me any trouble at all. I made it back to Smithers on the First of July, Canada's Independence Day.

I felt it was my own personal independence day. I was nearly a half a month into my walk and had survived that initial test in pretty good shape. I felt confident in my ability to make the whole journey, my ability to withstand hardship and physical exertion, and my own emotional equilibrium. It was nearly like being back on the SEAL Teams, even though I was alone. I was back to a place of solid strength like I had not felt since returning from Vietnam.

Later that day, I met a gentleman who owned a trailer park. His name was Walter Bucher. I talked to him for a while, and I pitched my tent in his trailer court and was able to take a shower there.

I was fairly certain at that time that my boots would arrive soon, so I thought I would just be spending a little more time in Smithers. As it worked out, I ended up spending a great deal more time there than I anticipated. Mail to that remote part of British Columbia in the mid 1970s was slow.

The man who owned the trailer park and his wife were pretty curious about my trip. They took me inside, sat me down, and we talked about it for quite some time. They gave me a big glass of fresh milk. They had their own cow out back, so the milk was exceptionally fresh. They were awfully nice people.

After having so many good experiences with kind souls, I was growing less leery talking to people. I had yet to meet anyone who wasn't interested in what I was doing or supportive of my goal. Still, I didn't tell people that I was walking from Alaska to Mexico. That was still just a little bit too much for most people to swallow. Jasper impressed them enough.

When I got up to go over to the campground, the Buchers gave me a quart of the milk from their cow to take with me. I pitched my tent, went over to the bathhouse for a good drink of water and a shower.

Walter Bucher, Jr. and his girlfriend Bonnie above Smithers.

Days were ticking by and I was really getting anxious to get my boots and head to Jasper. They didn't arrive on July 2. I had more time to kill.

That evening I got to meet the eldest son of Walter Bucher from the trailer park. Walter Jr. came over, introduced himself, and invited me over for dinner. I accepted the invitation. Like their dad, they had some questions about my trip. Spending time with Walter Jr., his girlfriend, her brother, and his friend was great. They were extremely nice people.

After dinner, we all drove up to an observation point in Walter Jr.'s van. It was one of the first clear days since I had arrived in Smithers. We looked to the south and saw the beautiful Hudson Bay Mountain Range and the Bulkley River coming down the valley. We also saw the Babine Mountain Range that formed the other side of the Bulkley Valley. It was

amazing to see that unbelievably green valley and the snowcapped mountains during the sunset. Fortunately I did get quite a few pictures of this area.

We then came back to their place after sunset, had a little more tea, and listened to John Denver and Gordon Lightfoot. We also had an enjoyable conversation about their lives. Walt Jr. told me that he wasn't just helping his dad with the camping area. He was a 22- year-old brakeman for the Canadian National Railroad, and his girlfriend, Bonnie, worked for the highway department. They also told me that Bonnie's brother, Les, and his friend Andy were just working there for the summer. It was a very special evening. I felt very much at home and at peace with these strangers who were becoming friends.

The next day, July 3, I still had not received my boots. I was trying awfully

53

hard to be patient. I did get a letter, though, from Mom. She let me know that the boots were on their way, but she didn't know when they were going to arrive. The forced idleness meant every day my feet were getting better and better. I had dinner that evening with Walt, Bonnie, and the crew again. It was a nice repeat of the night before.

The next day, July 4, was my happy Independence Day. The boots still hadn't arrived. I got so desperate that afternoon that I tried to order a pair of $100 boots through a local store. Unfortunately, that did not work either.

That evening, I met a gentleman by the name of Joe Watson who was living in the trailer park, too. He told me that he was the father of Joe and Jim Watson, professional hockey players for the Philadelphia Flyers in the States. His sons were in town conducting a hockey clinic at the Smithers Arena.

It had been raining off and on since I got back to Smithers. Fortunately, my tent had been working very well, so it was still comfortable. It looked like it was going to be a sunny the following day and my things would get a chance to dry out.

The sun was out July 5th, but I felt blue because still no boots. My feet were practically all healed up. I decided that my boots would get here when they get here, so I would just have to wait. That evening Walter, Sr. and his wife had me over to their place for a great spare rib dinner. I felt so lucky to be well-connected with this wonderful family.

On Saturday, July 6, my boots didn't arrive, but since it was another sunny day, Walt, Jr., Les, and I went for a run through the woods. It was great to get out and stretch again now that my feet were all healed up. Later on that afternoon, I met a friend and co-worker of Walt's from Jasper by the name of Rich, who also worked for the railroad and was being transferred to Smithers.

After we spent some time together, we all piled into Rich's and Walt's vans and went out to a place called McClure Lake for a great swim that afternoon. Instead of feeling sorry for myself, I enjoyed the workout and ensured that when my boots did arrive, I would be fit and ready to move on down the road. "Training is not over."

That evening we had fun going to a movie at the local drive-in and enjoyed having some popcorn. It ended being another wonderful day.

July 7th was a mellow Sunday. I spent most of the day getting my clothes cleaned. I was hopeful that tomorrow, I would finally have boots. That night, we all went out and had Chinese at a restaurant in Smithers. I got another restful night's sleep in my tent.

On Monday, July 8, the boots still didn't get there. I cannot begin to tell you how anxious I was to get on the move. I felt like I was living in Smithers. There was a carnival that came to town that evening, so the entire crew planned to go. While I was changing clothes in the tent that evening prior to going to the carnival, Walt's cat jumped up on the side of my tent and left a couple pretty good sized holes. Walt was very apologetic about that, but it didn't turn out to be too big a deal. I just patched it well enough to keep the rain out. We had a good time, and I dropped a couple bucks throwing baseballs.

Hallelujah! Early in the afternoon of July 9, my boots finally arrived. I was really glad to be able to continue the hike. My joy was mixed some regret. On the one hand, thank goodness, my journey would begin again. The arrival of my boots, on the other hand, meant that I would be leaving some pretty special people behind. I spent so much time in Smithers and made some good friends. Still, the road called.

By the time I got everything packed up and situated again, it was about 4:00 p.m. I left Smithers and headed for McClure Lake, the place where we had gone for that swim a few days previous. I ended up camping there at Provincial Park. The spot where I spent the night was only about 10 or 11 miles from Smithers. Since the boots were not very well broken in, I had a couple hot spots. I figured it was best to take my time until my feet and my boots were getting along better.

At about 3:00 a.m. that night, it began to rain hard. I hunkered down in my tent and hoped it would pass by morning. The sound of the raindrops pounding on the tent did not make for a very restful night. I was happy that my mending job from the damage Walt's cat had done was passing the test.

I waited for the weather to break in the morning, but it didn't. At about 9:00 a.m., I went out and grabbed breakfast from my pack that I left just outside of the tent and ducked back in and ate it. I then put my rain gear on, wrapped up, and packed up my tent and the rest of my gear. It was really a downpour, and there was no letup in sight. It was just grey from horizon to horizon. Everything that wasn't wet became wet in the pack. Sitting still wasn't going to make things better, so I decided to walk through the rain. I had been sitting enough the last week.

It ended up pouring continuously until about 3:00 p.m. that afternoon. I stopped at a little store along the way that morning and chatted with an elderly lady inside, mostly just to get out of the rain for a while. Like everyone I met along my way, she could not have been nicer.

My pack was becoming heavier and heavier through the day as it soaked up the rain. The day had started out pretty miserably, but it did change around 3:00 p.m. I stopped shortly thereafter to dry everything out. I laid things on a rock and ate a little late lunch. The bright sun worked pretty quickly on my damp gear.

After repacking my drier and lighter stuff, I hit the road again. A couple miles later, a guy pulled over and offered me a ride. I told him what I was up to. He congratulated me and just wished me luck. Every time someone did that, I felt a little bit better. I wondered at the power of words. When I came back from Vietnam, it only took a few mumbled words to cut me down. On the flip side, a honking horn and thumbs up lightened my heart.

Further along, I ran into a guy with a couple horses who was "packing;" traveling by horseback. He said that he had started in Williams, B.C., and was going up to the Yukon. He also told me about a dirt road shortcut from the main highway. It went by a place called Summit Lake, saving me approximately twelve highway miles.

That shortcut was damn near unbelievable: Grassy meadows bordered the little dirt road, clear streams cut across and along the path. Eventually, about six miles later, there glittered Summit Lake, as pretty a postcard view as ever you could want. I reached Summit Lake at nearly sundown. I crossed a meadow that went down right to the shoreline. The lake was surrounded by trees, with beautiful mountains off in the distance

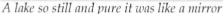

A lake so still and pure it was like a mirror

Sheep grazing in a mountain meadow.

reflected on its surface. I pitched my tent in the meadow and had dinner with a front row seat to that grandeur.

Just before turning in, I heard something bugle and rumble in the distance, and out of the woods came one of the biggest short-horn sheep bulls I've ever seen. He stopped about 30 feet from my tent. Fortunately, we were separated by a little bit of a gully. He snorted and pawed the ground as he looked at me and the tent. I grabbed the tent pegs and prepared to collapse the tent if it looked threatening enough to him that he would charge it, and then I would head for a tree. Fortunately, neither move was necessary. He bugled again and snorted a lot and finally headed on down the road. Peace

returned. I was exhausted and went to bed right after dinner.

Everything was still fairly damp from the prior rain. It didn't rain that night, so the tent did dry out a bit, but was still a little wet from the night before and the morning dew didn't help. That morning I wound up packing it damp again.

I had some oatmeal for breakfast the morning of July 11th and broke camp. Soon I started tracking my packer friend again. Since he had two horses, their tracks were fairly easy to distinguish among all the cow tracks in the mud—and the cow shit, too. There were a few forks in the road, but it wasn't too difficult to head in the proper direction, thanks to the packer

Grassy meadows surrounded by pristine meadows on my shortcut to the main highway.

and his horses. I came upon a ranch house about the time I figured I was only a couple miles from the highway. Outside that house, I talked to this guy who was helping his dad on their farm. He told me about a shortcut that was only a mile to the highway. I finally emerged on the main road at about 11:00 a.m.

The Lake Road shortcut turned out to be a time saver. As 2:00 p.m. rolled around on the highway, I was starting to get a bit hungry. Fortunately, I rounded a bend just up the road and came across a restaurant. It was a little campground restaurant combination-type place, so I ducked in there for lunch. It was great to get a good hot meal.

I made it to the town of Topley at about 4:30 that afternoon, and folks there told me about a little campground nine miles up the road. By this time in my hike, nine miles wasn't much.

I headed out for the campground, and the first two or three miles outside of Topley were just straight uphill. It did give my heels a couple hot spots, but no blisters. I lubed them up that night to prevent a problem the next day.

I reached a little summit later that afternoon and was heading out on the flat as an old pickup truck with about half a dozen kids in the back drove up next to me. It was heading in the opposite direction, because I was always walking on the left-hand side of the road into traffic for safety. As it got right beside me, the truck backfired.

"Incoming!"

Instantly, I was back in Vietnam. The explosion reminded me of mortars and rockets that regularly rained down on our compound.

Our base in Vietnam was in the Chuong Thien province that had a population that was 75% to 80% sympathetic to the Viet Cong. The people would smile at us as if they were friends, but then, with no warning, at any time of the day or night, you would hear a muffled "woof, woof," the sound of mortar launches from the neighborhoods surrounding our camp. Sometimes, you could see them coming in. Most times, you wouldn't hear or see anything until the exploding mortars hit. Then, it was too late to do anything but pray.

One time, we were gathered to watch a movie when a barrage of AK-47s began. Then someone shouted: "Mortar!" We ran to the nearest bunker as fast as we could. We would hunker down, crammed cheek to cheek, with no room to move for the 30 to 45 minute attacks, wondering if they would be followed by a storming of our walls by Viet Cong infantry. My job was to man the M60 in the event we were overrun. To say we went into high alert during these times is an understatement.

When the shelling stopped, I discovered the guy who had been sitting next to me at the movie had gotten killed. He couldn't fit all the way into the bunker and got hit by shrapnel. Things like that make you realize how random death can be and how little you personally can do to save yourself or anyone else when their number is up.

These attacks were constant, two or three a week. In seconds, you went from minding your own business to blinding terror, knowing there was nothing between you and death but sheer luck. Even today, a sudden loud noise sends my heart racing.

A lake high in the mountains.

Just as suddenly, I was back in the mountains of British Columbia. The pickup rattled on down the road, leaving me standing there. Luckily, I didn't dive into the ditch, but my heart rate didn't settle down for quite a while. My body and mind reacted like I was back in that hootch in Vietnam. I practiced deep breathing, a technique I had learned to help me control the panic and bring myself back to the present. After taking a few minutes to center myself, I took up my journey again and walked off the last bit of adrenalin in my system.

When I was only about two miles from the campground, a guy pulled over in another pickup and asked me if I wanted a ride. I explained to him that I was just walking. He asked if he could help me by carrying my pack or something and mentioned that I was near the campground and a good restaurant. That made me feel pretty good. I thanked him for the offer, but declined his help.

That ended a 28-mile day. On a wing and a prayer, I made it to Broman Lake Campground. I pitched my tent, and had an awfully good dinner. That night I called home to talk to Mom and Kevin, and that did my morale a world of good after the upsetting flashback that day. It was wonderful to hear their voices.

The following morning, July 12th, I had breakfast at the same restaurant. I only had 22 miles to go to a town called Burns Lake. About 12 miles into the day, I ran into a guy I had met while I was waiting for my boots in Smithers. He was riding his bicycle the same direction I was going. Stephan Gitchell and his wife were riding from Prince Rupert to Jasper, and then they were going to head south from there. I guess his wife got tired of riding for one reason or another. The weather didn't help. He ended up sending her home and was finishing the trip himself. I was glad that he was not in a big hurry. Since Burns Lake was his destination, too, he just walked his bike with me the rest of the way there. I enjoyed the company and the break from my solitude.

He and I both ended up setting up our tents in a little campground just outside of Burns Lake. It wasn't until later on that night, when we were having dinner, that we started talking about our

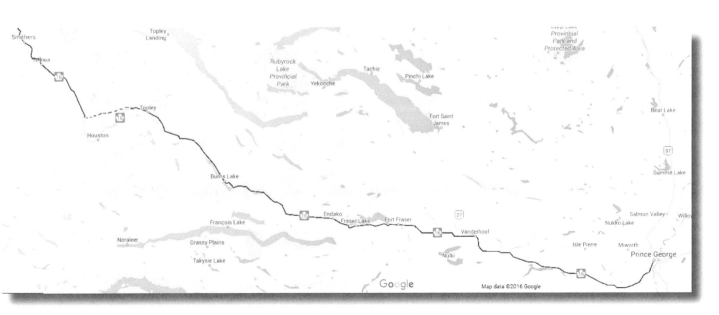

time in the military. It was the first time I had told anyone I had been to Vietnam since I started my hike. Stephan had served in the Marine Corps. We began to discuss where we were and when. Come to find out we had both been on the *USS Guam* when we went down to Peru in early 1970 to provide earthquake relief. We both considered that amazing, and here we were now both tripping through British Columbia together for a little while. What a small world! It felt good to be able to share stories with someone who understood and would not judge, even though I kept the disturbing ones to myself. I had gotten used to keeping a part of myself under wraps.

We each appreciated being able to get food and other supplies there before we left that Saturday morning, July 13th. Before Stephan rode off, he said that if I ever made it to Corvallis, Oregon, I should look him up. I told him I definitely would.

I lingered in the area a bit, deciding to take off later that day and maybe even layover one more day. It was such a great town and the campground had a shower. It was also a nice sunny day for resting. I ended up getting quite a bit done. I got all my clothes washed and was able to dry and lighten everything in my pack.

Later on, I went to a craft shop and bought some leather to make some insoles for my boots to help with my hot spots. It wasn't a very big deal because I didn't have any blisters, and the boots were nearly completely broken in, but I thought these would add a little insurance against future problems. I had broken in my previous boots and thought I put them through the test, only to have them fail me within days of starting the hike. I made my own insoles because I couldn't

find any ready-made insoles that were big enough for my boots.

I chatted with other folks at the campground. It struck me as interesting that the majority of people I ran into at that campground—and others—were Americans traveling east to west or west to east on bicycles, motorcycles or whatever. Since I was taking the slowest mode of travel, I felt like I got to meet everyone.

After having a couple good meals at Burns Lake, I relaxed by finishing the copy of Kurt Vonnegut's *Slaughterhouse-Five* that Buzz had left me. I had been burning through every chapter. Since I limited the things I carried, I had literally been using it for fire starter as I read it. I fell asleep at the end of that very productive, restful, and enjoyable day.

The morning of July 14th, I packed everything up and had a good breakfast. I wasn't in much of a hurry because there was supposed to be a campground at the end of the little ten-mile stretch.

Unfortunately, there wasn't, but there was a restaurant there. I had a good meal and I met some friendly people there. One of the guys had some land just adjacent to the restaurant, and he said that I was welcome to pitch my tent there. I spent the rest of the day catching up on my journal in the restaurant and staying away from the black flies that were pretty plentiful in that particular area. I took a close look at a map then, too, and figured out the mileage between where I was and Prince George. I figured if I got an early start the next morning, I could make it to a little town called Endako.

The refresh of the last two days made me ready on July 15th for an early start. I was up about 5:30 a.m., fixed breakfast, and was on the road by about 6:45. I thought I might be able to make it to Fraser Lake that day, 36 miles away. Unfortunately I endured two or three hours of steady, heavy rain that shortened my day, so I ended up staying in Endako as originally planned. It was a 28-mile day in about 8.5 hours including my breaks. Despite being ten miles under my goal, I was encouraged that my travel time was getting a little bit better. My feet were feeling good, and my boots were great.

Wet and tired, I checked into the Endako Hotel at 6:50 that night. It was a rather old hotel, but thank goodness it was dry. The bathroom was down the hall, so I took a warm bath in the tub, and that helped. The road to Endako was lined with marshes and poplars, not to mention the black flies. In one respect, the rain was a welcome treat because it did knock the bugs down.

During this point in the trip I was kind of running on a deferred gratification principle. The flats and the black flies were something to endure. I was very anxious to get to Mount Robson and the Jasper area to get back in the mountains again. I thought about getting beyond the flats, the marshes, and the bugs, which helped me pound out those miles. .

After getting a bath and getting myself cleaned up and dried out, I took everything out of my pack and hung it all over the room so my stuff would dry out by morning, too. Fortunately, it did.

July 16th was a beautiful morning. Everything was green and clean from the rain the previous day. The sky was just a solid blue as I headed east into the sun. According to the map, I would be traveling in an easterly direction until I got to Prince George. From there to Jasper would be mostly southeast.

Heading into the sun that morning, I decided to let breakfast wait until I got to Fraser Lake, about eight miles up the road. I got there about 10:45 a.m. and ate breakfast in a café in a shopping center. When I finished eating, I walked over to

Fraser Lake.

61

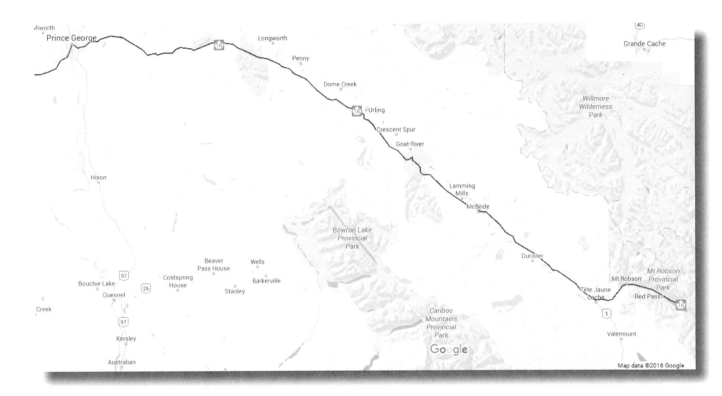

the grocery store at the other end of the shopping center and got some yogurt, milk, and some other snack things.

The next stop was Fort Fraser, about twelve miles away. Feeling full and pretty good after breakfast and some snacks, I didn't stop at all between Fraser Lake and Fort Fraser.

Coming into town that evening, I found a restaurant and ate dinner there. From talking to some people in the restaurant, I found out about a log church that a group of young people were living in about four miles down the road. The people in the restaurant suggested that would be a good place for me to camp that night, so I decided to go there.

I arrived a bit before dark and met the people who were living there, Bill and Debbie. They were both very warm and friendly, but they didn't quite know what to make of me and my trip. Still, they let me set up my tent on their property for the night. Bill and Debbie were both from Toronto and evidently were very tired of city living. They sure were doing without city comforts now! They didn't have any indoor plumbing in the log church, so all of their water had to be carried from the well out back. They had a nice garden, greenhouse, and some animals out back that were mostly pigs. They also had a goat that wandered around the church. He almost proved my undoing.

After I got my tent setup, the goat kept pawing at it and was trying to take a bite out of it. When I told Bill about this, I was glad that he decided to tie the goat up. I thanked him for using a real long, heavy-duty extension cord. They had a date that evening to go visit some friends and invited me to go along, but I was a little bit too tired. When they took off, I went to bed.

On July 17th, I woke up, packed up, and took off early in the morning. By 7:15 a.m., I was gone. About six miles up the road, I ran into a little oasis called the

View of the Rocky Mountains from Highway 16 in British Columbia, Canada.

Log Cabin Café. After having a fantastic breakfast and when I was almost ready to leave, I found out that the lady who made my meal turned out to be from Missoula, Montana. She hadn't been there for quite some time, but when she was in Missoula, she lived on Pattee Canyon Drive. That was the same street that my parents and younger brother lived on when Dad died in 1969. She said she hadn't been there for about ten years, so we had a nice chat about that. I took off shortly after our conversation and got back on the highway.

At about midday, I pulled into Vanderhoof, just ahead of the rain, which started when I got there for lunch. After lunch, I got ready for a cold, wet day. I changed into some long pants at a local gas station, packed up, and took off before the rain let up. Since it was very

grey outside, I assumed that it was going to rain for the rest of the day.

I climbed a hill just outside of Vanderhoof and after about three miles, I met an interesting elderly gentleman who was walking along the road, too. He had a rain slicker draped over one arm, and I stopped and chatted with him for a while. He told me he was 84 years old and walked at least ten miles every day, walked 20 miles frequently, and he'd even try 30 miles if someone would offer him a bet. He was quite an amazingly spry guy, probably the spriest older guy I had ever met. He attributed that to walking and herbs (he pronounced the "h" when he discussed herbs). He was really into herbal medicine and food. He was a really great fella.

I wound up staying about a mile down the road from where I met him at a trailer court and campground. It just so happened that this elderly hiker had a trailer there. I went over to see him after I got set up, and we had another little talk. He gave me some salve for my heels, which I didn't need then, but it did come in handy when I got back into the mountains. He told me that he was a native Canadian and that he had lived there his entire life. Since he still had hair on his head, I felt that that was worth bragging about.

The guy who owned the trailer park, Jim, was a nice guy, too. He suggested I get out of the weather. Rather than sleep in my tent, he let me crash in a little shed that he had by the restaurant. He also treated me to a pancake dinner.

I decided to just call it a day and enjoy a dry evening after about 24 miles. That night in the shed was not as restful as I had hoped. It was right beside a pump shed. Every 15 or 20 minutes this pump would kick on, rattle for about five minutes, and then shut down. It was a nice dry place to sleep, which I appreciated because it rained hard that night. I was glad to be inside. Still, I wished all night that I had had some ear plugs. I woke up with kind of a headache from that pump.

After leaving the shed, I caught a little breakfast at the restaurant and took off in the sunshine. I hadn't gone more than a couple miles when I ran across a guy who was just in the process of taking down his tent by the side of the road. His ten-speed bike was leaning up against a nearby telephone pole. He introduced himself as Ron Haddad from Brooklyn, New York. He was biking from New York City to Prince Rupert on the Pacific Coast. He said he had been riding for about seven weeks and hoped to catch the ferry to Alaska once he got to Prince Rupert. He was planning to stay in Alaska for a little while before flying home. He said he had been riding with a friend of his, but somewhere between Banff and Jasper, his friend had cut his hand pretty badly and was forced to go back home. Ron was now in the process of finishing the trip by himself. He wasn't too sure where in Alaska he wanted to go; he was just going to get up there and see how it went. I gave him Walter's address in Smithers, so he would have a place to camp there.

After Ron and I said goodbye, a pair of bikers came riding up behind me. They introduced themselves as Pete Vogel and Jack Steinhorst from Colorado. As we were talking there by the side of the road, a camper drove up and pulled over, and it was Pete's folks. I guess they had been on the coast vacationing and fishing for a while, so we chatted with them. It was kind of like a reunion there in the middle of the road. We were all headed for Jasper, but I was traveling a lot slower than everyone else.

I grabbed a 7-Up at a place called Beaver Campground, and I talked to a lady there who said that about nine miles up the road was a place called Bednesti where I could find a campground, truck stop, and restaurant. I figured that if I could make it there by the end of the day, it would be about a 30-mile day. When I looked at the map, I calculated it would put me within shooting distance of Prince George the next day.

A few miles from the campground, I put my pack down for a second and checked and made sure I hadn't dropped something. As I swung it back on, I didn't realize that I knocked my leather bracelet off my wrist. It was given to me by a close friend, Ken Staninger, before I left Missoula. Unfortunately, I didn't realize that I had lost the bracelet until I was about three miles down the road. When I looked on my wrist and had no bracelet, I knew exactly where I lost it a few miles back by the road.

Frustrated, I took my pack off, hid it by the road, and then ran down the hill back to the bracelet. All the way back, I kept thinking of how stupid I was not to notice that I had knocked it off. I backtracked and finally found it. I then ran back up the hill to where my pack was. I was glad I couldn't see my pack from the other side of the hill; I had hid it well.

By the time I got back to the pack, I was disgusted and tired, and my patience was almost shot. It turned out that wasn't one of my better days. I decided at that point, when I finally got my pack back on, that since I had run a backtrack of about five or six miles, if anybody offered me a ride, just then, I would take exactly a three-mile ride. Thankfully, someone did offer me a ride, and I took it. Oddly enough, the guy who picked me up was Bob Aldridge, a relative of Tim Aldridge whom I played some ball with in Missoula. Bob now owns a hunting lodge in British Columbia. It was quite a coincidence.

I got out of the car exactly three miles down the road, in the middle of nowhere. Bob couldn't quite understand that, but he congratulated me for what I was doing. It was nice getting to meet and talk to someone from Missoula and resting for a few miles.

Even though I made up more of the miles and hadn't cheated one single step, I told myself this was going to be my very last ride. I felt a little disappointed in myself for taking that ride, because hardship was part of the journey. At that moment, though, I was too tired to worry about it.

About an hour later, I rolled into Bednesti. As promised, there was a truck stop, campground, and motel by a small lake, complete with mosquitos. After I had my dinner, I got my tent about half set up, when it started to hail strongly for about 30 minutes. Then the rain started. By the time I got my tent set up, it was soaked inside and out, so I decided to shell out 10 bucks for a dry room. That night, I was able to get all my gear dry again.

On July 19th after breakfast, I got on the road again a little after 9:00 a.m. and was going to try to make it to Prince George that day. Weather-wise, it was a mixed day. It would rain for a little while, and then it would clear up and be just beautiful for a little while, and then it would rain again. It never got too cold, so the rain was not a big deal. I made it to Prince George around 9:30 p.m. It had been about a 35-mile day, my longest one so far.

On the way, I met some highway construction workers who were picking wild strawberries alongside the road, so I joined them and they shared that welcome treat. They were also impressed with the way I was traveling and the fact that I started in Alaska and was headed for Jasper, Alberta.

It took a few sets of wrong turns to make it to the hostel in town. Since it was so late, all that was left was floor space. It was only 75 cents a night, so I couldn't complain too much. I had a roof over my head at least. Once I got checked in, I stashed my pack and went over to the Colonel's Chicken and had dinner. I met some nice people there, but that was the first and the last hostel that I stayed in while traveling through Canada. They were not convenient to my route and they tended to shut for the night too early for me.

I was truly exhausted from that day, so I decided to stay in Prince George until Monday. On July 20th, the next morning, I ate my French toast as the complimentary breakfast that goes along with a hostel thing. I then packed up and headed for town to try to find a cheap hotel or motel room if I could. Sleeping on their floor was not for me.

Fortunately, it didn't take me too long to find a reasonable place, the Canada Hotel. My room was small, clean, dry, and away from the bugs. It was perfect. The remainder of that day was spent running around town buying things I needed for the next leg of the trip and washing clothes. I also made up a package of different things I figured I

would not need for a while and boxed them up and mailed them home. Before I had started this hike, I had taken a course on Eastern religions. Now that I was done with Vonnegut, I needed something to read on the road. I bought a copy of the *Bhagavad Gita*. That evening after dinner, I felt good and went to bed early.

July 21st was Sunday. I got up at about 8:45 a.m., had some breakfast and then called home. I was very lucky to catch my brother Kevin and talk to him for a while. I had not been homesick, but still it was great to hear his voice and find out what and how he was doing this summer.

It was a beautiful Sunday, so I grabbed some bread and cheese and decided to head for Connaught Park, which sits up on a hill right in the middle of the city. The view from there was great,

Bear grass in the mountains.

and I enjoyed a picnic and a little reading in the park.

After the park visit, I promised myself a steak and a movie that night. *The Spikes Gang* with Lee Marvin was the first movie I had seen in weeks and I enjoyed it. When I got back to the hotel, I packed up some of my stuff that night so I could get going early and went to bed.

July 22nd, Monday, I left Prince George pretty early. My feet now were so callused over and my boots were so well-broken-in that I wasn't even getting any hot spots any more.

It sprinkled a bit as I left town, but it was nothing very serious. I felt ready and energized to put some miles behind me. I ended up getting breakfast about four miles out of town. Since it was a nice, warm day, I also stopped in a place called Tabor Lake to change into my shorts. It was evidently a little Norwegian settlement because I saw a sign that that said, "Sons of Norway Recreation Area," and it pointed down to the lake. My uncle Chjald (Norwegian for Charles) Lorentzen, Ivan and Chuck's dad, would have gotten a kick out of it. He was from Norway and belonged to The Sons of Norway in Kalispell, Montana.

Just before I got to my planned stopping point at Willow River, I passed through an area where they were doing road construction work. One of the construction guys stopped and gave me a beer that I thanked him for. I just got my tent up before the rain started, so I was able to stay dry all night. I studied my map and realized I was about 225 miles from Jasper. I went to bed fairly early that evening before it was even dark, and got a great night's sleep.

On July 23rd, I was up at 6:00 a.m. and on the road. I made it to Purden Lake by 11:30 and had some lunch there. Judging from the map, it looked like the lake was the only notable spot between Prince George and a little town of McBride. The whole place consisted of a little restaurant and a filling station. A sign there said 90 miles to the next services. I guessed that meant it was 90 miles to McBride. That section of road was pretty flat, with muskeg swamp off to the side, which made the mosquitos pretty plentiful. I was eager to put it behind me.

At about 4:00 p.m. that afternoon, I came upon an older couple stopped by the side of the road having lunch. They were extremely warm folks. Toby and Tina Cappola were from Finland originally, and they currently lived in southern British Columbia, not too far from the Washington State border. Now they were just traveling around exploring the area in their little VW Bug with a tent they would set up at night. They gave me a couple open-face sandwiches, a cup of coffee, a few sweet rolls, and a couple oranges for the road. We bonded over being Scandinavians. They were glad to hear about my Norwegian background. I thanked God for bringing these wonderful folks and their food into my trip! It was wonderful to feel so welcomed and accepted.

It was a beautiful sunny day, and I ended up making camp quite a bit before sunset by a picturesque mountain stream that flowed under the road. The hills were getting higher and higher as I got closer and closer to McBride. I kept hoping I would be in the mountains before too long. From where I stopped, I could see snowcapped mountain peaks off in the distance, and I was getting very anxious to get there. Just being able to see them did me a world of good. I started to eat dinner by the stream and was still pretty full, thanks to Toby and Tina. But it wasn't too long before the mosquitos found me and drove me into the tent. That day wound up to be about a 30-miler.

On July 24th, I was on the road by 7:00 a.m. I packed up pretty quickly and was getting into the routine of finishing breakfast fast. I would eat a big bowl of granola because it stuck with me for quite a while.

I ran into road construction again during the first couple miles that morning. That made the road pretty dusty for a while, and then it started to sprinkle, which helped keep the dust down. Whether it was raining or not, I would get an average of about three to six ride offers a day. To all of them, I'd explain briefly what I was up to.

Soon after my last offer, I came upon another road construction area. One of the flag girls asked me if I was the guy who was walking from Alaska to Montana. When I told her I was, she told me that I was a couple days late. I apologized, and we both laughed. She said that one of the people who had stopped to pick me up had stopped to talk to her and told her about me.

I put in about a 13-and-a-half hour day altogether. I made camp near a creek there, and I saw a sign that indicated I was now 90 miles out of Prince George. When I made camp by this stream, I became determined to make it to McBride by the next night. The mountains were calling to me and I longed to be up among those peaks. That meant that the next day would be a 40 to 45 mile day. That would be farther than I had ever traveled in one

The beauty of the mountains made this place feel sacred.

day before, so I felt that it should prove challenging.

On July 25th, I was up at 5:30 a.m. It had been a chilly night and it still was that morning. The good news was that there were no mosquitos. Obviously, the cold took those little buggers out the night before. I appreciated that. I remember reading some place, an old Chinese proverb that stated in effect, "If heaven made it, then the earth will find a place for it." I tried very hard to determine how that could apply to mosquitos and black flies, especially for someone like me who spent so much time outside.

Every day was bringing me closer to the mountains. It was beautiful now that I could see them.

I started at about 6:00 a.m. that morning and decided to walk at a three-mile-an-hour pace all day and to stop as few times as possible. I knew if I was going to make that many miles, it was going to be a long day. I stopped briefly at about 12:30 next to a river running by the road near a pretty big bridge. I had some crackers with peanut butter and jelly on them and a few of the other things that I had left over. I figured that would keep me going until McBride anyway, and fortunately it did.

I rolled into McBride at dusk about 9:45 p.m. It was damned near a 16-hour day. During the last few miles into McBride, it seemed to be kind of an elusive city. It was one of those things that from the terrain and the houses and everything, it looked like McBride would be right around the corner. I walked on for about four miles thinking I was close, but McBride never seemed to be around the corner. By the time I made it into town, I was so tired that it felt like my legs were moving on their own, and I was

just perched on top of them. "Training is not over." Thank you, Chief Byers for reminding me of that.

I was cordially welcomed at the McBride Hotel for $12.60 a night for a single room with the bathroom down the hall. The gal at the desk assured me this was the best and least expensive place in town. I went up to my room and dropped my pack off. I then shuffled over to a place called the Alpine Café and proceeded to eat enough to fill the table with empty plates. After dinner, I took a quick shower. Because I was so tired, I went right to bed.

In the morning, I woke up in exactly the same position that I went to sleep in. I figured I earned a rest and decided to stay in McBride to complete some errands. I washed my clothes, bought some extra food. After a nap, I caught up on my journal and got together with a map and calculated that I was about 105 miles away from Jasper at this point. That night, I went to sleep early, and even though there was a little noise in the room next door, I got a great night's sleep.

On July 27th, I woke up that morning and ate breakfast in the hotel dining room and was on the road by about 9:30 a.m. I decided to hike in my track shoes. The soles of my boots were becoming pretty badly worn. I just hoped they would last until Jasper. Walking day after day in a good bit of rain, the boots had never really had a chance to dry out completely, so they stayed damp and pliable, which had been great. I was worried that the soles of my boots didn't have that many days left on them, and I wanted to be able to use them as many days as possible before getting to Jasper.

Once there, I was going to have them resoled.

About mid-afternoon, two young ladies came over the hill riding bicycles heading in the opposite direction I was. One stopped to talk to me. Linda Sue Salmon and her friend had pedaled all the way from California and were on their way to Prince Rupert, where they planned to catch the ferry to Alaska. They were awfully anxious to get to McBride.

Interestingly, they met Pete and Jack, the cyclists I had met outside of Vanderhoof, in Jasper and spent some time with them. What a small world! Linda Sue and I had a nice little chat, and then we both wished each other well on our trips and headed in our different directions. They were the only women whom I had met so far who were doing anything like that.

As I got about 25 miles down the road outside of McBride, I heard someone hollering at me. I looked over, and two people were waving from a log farm house that was about a hundred yards off the road. A couple of youngsters, a girl and her younger 18-year-old brother rode over on bicycles to say hello. We chatted for a while in their driveway. They confirmed that we were 25 miles from McBride. It seemed like a good stopping place, so I asked if I could talk to their folks about pitching my tent in their yard that night.

The Lorenze family was extremely friendly. The father, a traveling tool salesman, said I could stay and invited me to come in for dinner. Then we all piled into the family pickup and drove about six miles down the road to a little store and bought some ice cream and doughnuts. After returning to their home we chatted until it was time for everybody

to go to bed at about 10:00 p.m. I thanked them for their hospitality. They had made me feel so welcome. I told them that, since I was anxious to get to McBride, I would probably be gone by the time they got up in the morning.

On July 28th, I was up very early in the morning and gone by about 7:00 a.m. I was very glad that I had had a chance the night before to thank the Lorenzes before I left. A couple hours later, I rolled into the same store we had ice cream in the night before and had my breakfast there.

The sun was shining and the daisies were nodding in the breeze. I was so glad I was to be into the beautiful mountains. I also relished being able to drink the cold mountain stream water. As much as I liked the company of the people I met along the way, I also enjoyed my solitude. Alone, I could soak in the smell of the different flowers along the road, marvel at the beauty of the songs of each species of bird, and hear the steady crunch of my boots on the road. I didn't have a Walkman or MP3 player, just the world around me and my own thoughts. Walking was a form of meditation for me. I thought about how free I felt starting the trip in Alaska, and now, well into it, I was freer still.

When I got to Tete Jaune Junction, I had a 7-Up at a hotel in town. As I was leaving, I ran into a guy from Minnesota who was hitchhiking. He was headed west and was quite a character. He had a lobster tan, half a beard like I did, and wore shorts and tennis shoes. He was eating a chunk of Philadelphia cream cheese like a candy bar and wearing some on his beard. Since he had a Navy hat on, I asked him if he had been in the service. He said he hadn't; he had just gotten it at a surplus store. I didn't share with him

locked inside, I went back into my tent and sleeping bag and got some more rest and did a little *Bhagavad Gita* reading until they opened up.

A little before 7:00 a.m., I heard some action inside, so I knocked on the window. I thanked Jerry and Fred was his 21-year- old son for saving me from the bear. Since I was safe, I wasn't so concerned about getting my early start. It was a fair tradeoff.

"Ode to a Travelin' Hat"
Mine has fanned many dying camp fires
And shed many driving rains
It's battered and it's filthy
But I love it just the same
Now hunger and cold are facts of the road
But what's even worse than that
Would be, to be on the road a traveling
Without a travelin' hat!
—GB

that I was a vet. I took off so I wouldn't scare his rides away.

As I headed out and around a corner, I could see Mount Robson right in front of me. It was really spectacular. I was lucky to be able to spend that night in Mount Robson Park at the base of the mountain. There was a little café called the Mountaineer Take-Out and a filling station. I met Jerry who owned the place who let me pitch my tent there. They also let me use their phone to call Mom and Kevin at home. As always, that was wonderful. After calling home, I updated my journal.

Before I went to bed, the folks at the Take-Out told me that there had been a bear in the area not long ago, so they let me lock my pack inside the building that night. Early in the morning, I heard the bear rattling around in a nearby garbage can. When I got up and went outside of my tent, I noticed that many of the local garbage cans had been turned over. Thank God, the bear wasn't interested in me or my tent!

On July 29th, I had every intention of getting an early start. I was up at 5:30 a.m., but since the Mountaineer Take-Out was not open yet and my pack was

Jerry and I had a nice chat about hiking, and Fred started fixing both of us a great bacon and eggs breakfast. After our meal, Jerry and I continued talking over coffee. They wouldn't let me pay for my breakfast, so I thanked them for that, too, and took off.

It was about 9:00 a.m. by then and a beautiful morning when I headed up the hill. I reached a little stream soon after I left, and before it ran under the highway, it formed a little pool. Sweaty as I was, I put my pack down, shed my shirt, and took an upper body bath in the cool pool. Thank goodness it was a pretty warm day for me to get a bit cleaner. I let the sun dry me off as I ate my lunch. Earlier Jerry had told me about a place called Lucerne Campground that was around 30 miles from where I started that morning, so I decided to shoot for that.

Walking along, I felt such a feeling of achievement together with a sense of peace. I was a quarter way through the hike. Though I had many miles ahead of me, I had covered considerable emotional ground.

I was really joyful about being back in the mountains. I always felt more spiritually connected to God, the Creator, in the mountains. I was fortunate to have been raised in the Flathead Valley, in the mountains of western Montana. Growing up as a Lutheran, I was always fascinated by Mount Sinai. At the University of Montana, I took a comparative religion class and was moved by the "sacred sites" in all religions, including many Eastern Orthodox religions and Native American spirituality.

This day in the mountains felt sacred, especially near sunset, which was extremely beautiful. I had been looking at these mountains for days, longing to be in them, and now I was. I was also reading books on Eastern Religions, including the *Bhagavad Gita*, and as I walked that got me thinking about sacred places like this one.

That one day, late in the afternoon, I came over a hill, and I was awestruck by the view. The mountains were bright gold, the sun was setting. The Frasier River was as flat as a mirror, flowing into the long shadows cast by overhanging trees, almost looking as if it were slipping down into the earth. As I was greeted by this view on the crest of that hill, I saw a sign that said "Gita Creek." The connection with what I had been reading and what I was now viewing started me crying. Here I was, weeping, and thinking I was going nuts, but it felt so good I didn't want it to stop.

At that moment, I felt that the trail, my current trip, was spiritually reinforced and approved of. I had another feeling that, like my journey up to this point, enlisting in the Navy, volunteering for UDT training, and going to Vietnam were all approved of as well. I thought: "Oh, my God, that's wonderful!"

I thought about all the ugly words said to me and about me and my fellow veterans when I returned from Vietnam. I marvelled at the power of words to hurt and destroy. What right did any of these people have to say these things? If I was listening to them, I was listening to the wrong voices.

Before I was done with my hike that day, a thought occurred to me—I didn't hear it in a voice—it simply came to mind: "Teach without Teaching." At the time, I didn't know what it meant, but I never forgot it. It would only be years later that it would become clear. I did think about the power of words and thought then that I would use my words to build back up what the words of other people had tried to destroy.

I had a small smile for myself. When I started the hike, a Bob Dylan lyric was stuck in my head. I had so many questions then, and now, I felt the answer had come to me blowing in the wind there on that blustery trail in the mountains.

After all this, I finally got to Lucerne Campground. The sun had set, and it was dark by then. The sign outside the campground said it was filled up, but I walked in anyway figuring that because it was filled with campers and motor homes, I could probably find a place to pitch my tent.

I saw a couple sitting in front of their Winnebago and campfire and went up and just started chatting with them. One thing led to another, and they invited me to pitch my tent on their pad and spend the evening there. They were very nice people; he was a fireman from Edmonton. They also treated me to dinner, gave me a couple beers, and a bunch of goodies. It wasn't too long after that we all went to bed.

On July 30th, when I got up that morning, I was pretty excited because I knew I would be getting to Jasper, Alberta, that day since it was only about 22 miles away. After breakfast, I took off at about 7:00 a.m. I made it to the British Columbia/Alberta border at about 9:00 a.m. I was taking a picture at the border when a guy riding his bicycle in the opposite direction stopped to talk for a while. He was in his late 60s, was in pretty amazing shape, and also had a beautiful bike. His story was that he and his wife were from Oregon, they were vacationing in Jasper, and he was taking just a 15-mile ride to loosen up that morning. Later, about 11:30, I stopped by a river and ate. I got into Jasper at about 2:45 p.m. That day I saw a number of people on the highway trying to hitchhike into Jasper without much luck.

CHAPTER 4
Hiking Jasper to Waterton

One of the people I had met during my extended stay waiting for boots in Smithers with Walter was his daughter Debbie. She was an 18-year-old gal who lived in Jasper at a place called the Fort Point Lodge. She had come to visit Bonnie while I was in Smithers, so I got to know her a bit. When I got to Jasper, the first place I headed for was the Fort Point Lodge.

I was able to find a safe place at the Lodge to leave my pack so I could go find Debbie. I planned to ask her where in town would be a good place for me to stay and rest for a few days. Folks at the Lodge told me she was at work at the Jasper Camera and Gift Shop and gave me directions for getting there. When I found Debbie, she told me she was living in an apartment with three other girls. She invited me to sleep on the living room floor of their apartment, since Jasper's free campground was already filled up. I remembered talking to Walter and Debbie's sister Bonnie when I was in Smithers (they lived in Jasper for a while)

about the free camp. They said that during certain times of the year the camp was really kind of a neat place. It's just like a little city. Unfortunately, that time of year, there were just too many people for me to be able to find a spot.

Things turned out well with me staying in Debbie's apartment. I don't have any sisters, but I felt like I did in Jasper for a few days. And I was glad to have a roof over my head and be able to buy them some food.

Jasper is kind of a miniature Banff in a lot of ways. It's pretty commercialized and it has become a year-round tourist destination. Ski resorts operate in the winter, and in the summer, there's a lot of mountain hiking activity and tourism in general. It's a very scenic area in the mountains.

The soles of my boots were pretty well filed down by the time I got to Jasper. I was lucky they made it that far. The project the next day, the 31st of July, was to get my boots fixed. I found out that the nearest boot repair shop was in Hinton, a town about 45 miles away. I decided to try to hitchhike to Hinton, and Debbie said she would go with me. Even with her beside me, we still didn't get picked up. We tried for a couple hours until I realized it was hopeless. I thanked her and decided to ride the local bus by myself from Jasper to Hinton.

When I got to Hinton's shoe repair shop, I explained to the guy there what I needed to have done and how important it was that the soles stay on the boots for at least another 500 miles. He said that he would not only fix my boots for me, but also that he had a guy who would bring them to a local printing shop in Jasper so I would not have to take another long bus ride. I was intrigued by what he said he

was going to do. He said he would use the tread from a car tire, explaining that the rubber would make each step softer, even though they made each boot heavier. And he guaranteed they would really last. After paying and thanking him for that, I caught another bus back to Jasper.

After I got back to town, I invited my "sisters" out to a spaghetti dinner that night and washed some of my clothes. Later, I had a good night's sleep.

August 1st was a beautiful, sunny day. That morning, I put some ice in plastic bags on my knees and ankles. The highway system in Alberta is extremely good if you happen to be driving a car or riding a bicycle, because there is another lane that is paved on the shoulder. If you happen to be walking on this pavement, it is rather hard on your knees and ankles because there is no dirt shoulder to cushion your steps.

I went out and caught some rays that afternoon. I really enjoyed having a good place to rest, access to good food, and not having to move very much for a while. I was a bit underfoot in the apartment at night because there was quite a bit of traffic in there then. Fortunately, the gals didn't mind. It was a relaxing day and a beautiful evening.

On August 2nd, I talked to a guy by the name of Brian Dill who worked for the Canadian National Railroad. He was a hiker who had spent a lot of time on the trails around Jasper. I'm glad we met because I wanted to find out about the trail system between Jasper and Banff. He told me about a route that went south of Jasper, the very famous Skyline Trail, and its amazing scenery. He recommended that I start on that one, but he warned me that the trails don't go all the way to Banff. I talked to some wardens and made some arrangements to begin my hike south on the Skyline Trail on Sunday morning, August 4th. With those plans made, I began buying groceries and other supplies and getting packed up and ready to leave. Fortunately, my boots arrived that afternoon. I had been enjoying my stay in Jasper a lot, just walking around town, resting, and hanging out with my "sisters."

August 3rd, a Saturday, Debbie and a girlfriend of hers by the name of Roseanne left for a weekend in Edmonton, so I moved out of their apartment and moved in upstairs with another gal, Karen, a friend of Debbie's, who I had met in the Fort Point Lodge. I stayed on the floor in her apartment, for just one day and night. I was very grateful for her hospitality, too.

I went to see the park warden that afternoon to confirm that I was heading out the next morning and to find out about the procedure for checking in and out of the trails. I filled out a form and checked into the trail for the morning of the 4th, Sunday. That Saturday evening, I went downtown and had dinner, marveling that the town was so crowded.

I got up early the next morning, August 4th, and had a good pancake breakfast before I took off. I was on the road by about 7:00 a.m. The map that I had wasn't very specific, so I had an extremely difficult time finding the beginning of the Skyline Trail. The road where the trail started wasn't marked at all. It turned out that this was just the beginning of a long hassle with poorly marked trails and roads in the Canadian parks.

My pack resting next to a fast-moving river down from the mountains.

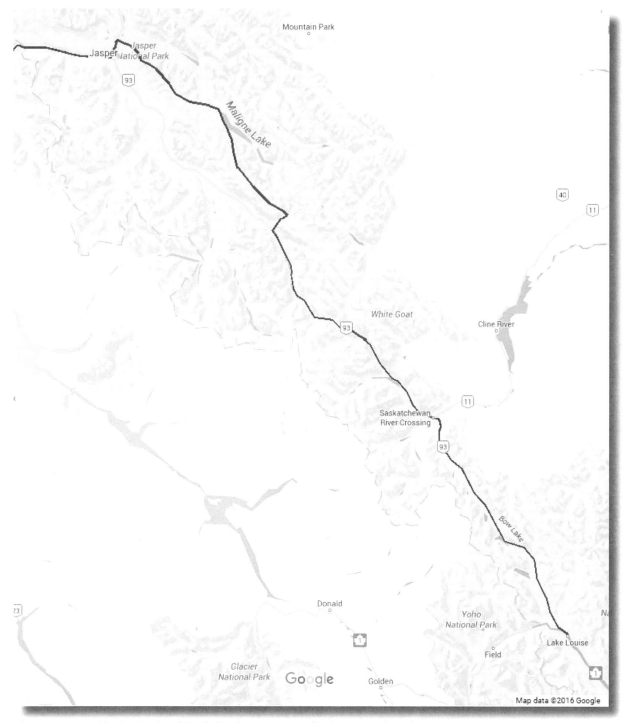

I saw signs to Glacier National Park, but knew I was still a long way from home. Canada's GlacierNational Park is nowhre near Montana's Glacieir National Park.

Luckily, I ran into two couples who happened to be hiking up a different road to a look-out where the trailhead I was looking for started. If it hadn't been for them, I would have ended up staying on the wrong road all the way to Maligne Lake, missing the trail completely. As it went, I backtracked with them and walked up that switchback for about eight miles and got to the head of the trail. Thank goodness!

We reached the trailhead at about 11:00 a.m. Skyline was a good name for that trail because it was almost at the tree line. It was just a beautiful day. The sun was shining, and once I got up to that elevation, I could look back and see the town of Jasper and the Athabasca River. It was really a pretty view. I found out later from some hikers going the other way that the normal route for taking the Skyline Trail starts at Maligne Lake. People go that way because the vertical rise is a little less. They assured me that I would really enjoy my hike because the view remained spectacular.

Once I got above the tree line, the trail followed a ridge, and the whole Canadian Rockies opened up to me. I stopped at the first of three major campgrounds on the trail and ate my lunch of dried fruit and sunflower seeds. I thought of my moment a few days back at Gita Creek and thanked God for the beauty before me.

I had to ford a stream just prior to getting there, so I had to take my boots off, wear my track shoes, and then wring my socks out. There were a number of streams on this trail, due to the elevation and that most of the trail was snow packed until a short time previous to my arrival. Some of the streams were a bit swollen, and there were no hiker fords over any of them. Most of the streams I could just skip across or pick my way from rock to rock. Still, I got wet more than once any way.

As I gained elevation, the wind got stronger and stronger. The sunshine and the scenery more than made up for it. As I came over the first rise, they called The Notch, the whole range of the Canadian Rockies was visible. Off in the distance, I could see Mount Robson, followed by one

magnificent peak after another. The wind up there was very brisk. I was taking a few pictures with my sunglasses on. I turned my head sideways, and the wind whipped my sunglasses off and blew them downslope about a hundred feet. I took my pack off and backtracked to get down to them. After retrieving my shades and coming back up over the top of The Notch, I talked to a few people there at the summit and then continued on.

The trail from there skirted a rock slide and went up and over another notch and came to a cornice of snow. This was one of the critical danger areas and was the reason they hadn't opened the trail earlier. By the time I got there, the cornice had had enough traffic over it that steps were cut into it. It was still a bit slick in some spots, but I got down it safely. And the view remained magnificent.

I descended a short stretch of trail from the cornice, and it led me to a little crater lake that was glacier-fed at that elevation. It was a pretty windy spot, both strong and gusty. The day was still early, around 5:30 in the afternoon, but it was a good place to stop. I was pretty tired because I had put in about 25 miles or so that day, and a lot of them involved climbing. I settled down to have a little dinner.

I figured I would set my tent up first. I tried to find an area that was a little sheltered from the wind. I found a spot where the wind was not too strong, but it was still gusting pretty fiercely. I was determined to test the wind-ability of my tent and the 6- to 8-inch stakes that I had. I staked the back down into the wind gusts, put a big rock on it, and started to draw the front up with the arches already in it. As I gently pulled the front and knelt down to put those stakes in, a strong gust of wind picked the tent up out of my hands and blew it down a short cliff studded with very sharp rocks. It rolled and landed in this damned glacial lake. I scrambled down the cliff and ran after it as it caught some air and quickly drifted out away from the shore. After feeling the temperature of the water, I also realized I would need to take the time to get naked to swim after it. And as I was considering that, the tent was already nearly halfway across the lake. At that temperature, I knew it was going to be a life-threatening swim, so I felt like that certainly wasn't the answer.

Then a very bizarre thing happened to me. I stood a moment by the side of the lake, watching my tent getting smaller and smaller, but then started running around the lake, praying that the tent would stay afloat until it reached the far side. I arrived there before the tent did, feeling helpless, watching and hoping that the tent would not sink before it got to where I was standing. If I would have had my wits about me, it would have made a great picture, but the last thing I had on my mind was running for the camera at that point.

The far side of the lake consisted of big rocks that had broken off the mountainside, which was straight up from the lake itself. I watched the bubble keeping the tent afloat get smaller and smaller. Those 30 to 45 minutes seemed like an eternity, but, miraculously, my tent finally got over to my side of the lake. I could see it had holes in it from the cliff as I fished it out. Luckily, it was a double-layer tent. It had so much water in it that it was just like a sea anchor. I took out the stays, dumped the water, and held it up to the wind to let it whip dry for the most part. I then rolled it up around the stays,

tucked it under my arm, and went back to where my pack was. I cussed myself all the way back for even trying to set it up in that high wind.

A little disgruntled, I fixed dinner, and ended up making a kind of hap-hazard shelter out of my ground cloth in a dried-up runoff ditch. That set-up in the dry, gassy little dip got me out of the direct wind and proved to be pretty cozy, since the wind kept blowing and providing enough ventilation that condensation wasn't a problem. After all that, I finally got a good night's sleep.

The next morning, August 5th, the wind woke me up early. I fixed a makeshift breakfast and took off. The sun was just barely hitting the tops of the peaks. It was a beautiful, but chilly morning because the wind was still blowing hard in that valley. I picked my way up and over a formation called Shovel Pass, then went down the other side into a lush, green valley. The sun was a little higher by then, and my elevation had decreased. The wind died down some, and it was warmer. I had a few challenging, swollen creeks to cross, so I welcomed the increased temperature.

It was quite some time before I met anybody coming the other way on the trail, about mid-morning. There are only a few designated camping spots along the trail, and the wardens preferred that everyone use those. After crossing a few of these streams, I came to a place called Snowbowl Campground. I met three young couples there who were emerging from their tents, cussing and slapping at the mosquitos when I arrived. Evidently, the campground was a pretty mosquito-ridden spot. They told me that they didn't get much sleep, which was why they all looked so tired. I asked them if they had brought any insect repellant, and they hadn't. Since I had about a bottle and a half of Cutter repellant, I gave them the half bottle, for which they were very thankful and quite relieved.

From there, it was just up and over another little pass, and then was all downhill from there to Maligne Lake. I wound up getting to Maligne Lake at approximately mid-afternoon. I was hungry enough to get a late lunch at a local café.

After eating all that I could, I went over to the warden's office to ask him about the trails and the campgrounds. In Canada, they call their park rangers wardens. I was going to follow the Continental Divide trail from there south through Jasper Park. I wanted to get a little more detailed information from him about this route. While I was waiting for this warden to come back to his office, I unpacked my tent and took a close look at the new holes in it. I set it up and took out my ripstop tape and started to go to work on repairing it in the warden's front yard.

When the warden came back, he told me I couldn't camp in the Maligne Lake area, but suggested a little campground on Trapper Creek about six miles up the trail. Since that was the way I was headed anyway, I packed up and took off.

After I got to the Trapper Creek Campground, I set up my tent near a party of about seven or eight Canadians who were hiking the other direction down the trail. The man and his wife were in their 50s, traveling with their adult kids who were in their 20s and 30s. It was a neat evening spending time with the spry, older couple and their nice kids. They gave me a lot of valuable information

Ridge along Skyline Trail.

Snow field along the trail.

about the trail ahead. They also told me that I was a few days behind a train of about 29 horses, which was helpful later in my hike. It was easy to lose the trail when I would come to a meadow. The horses had apparently fanned out, and the trail would disappear. The leader of the horse pack knew where the trail was on the other side of the meadow, but I didn't since there were no signs. My eyes might lose the trail, but my nose never did, thanks to the horse crap. The folks I was camping with that night also told me about following some llama crap at one point. That was kind of interesting. I imagine it was a little startling to round the corner, see four packing llamas, and think you really took a wrong turn some place.

On August 6th, I got another early start at about 7:30 a.m. A bit later, I had my first major river ford. I'm not certain what the name of the river was, but I think it was just the Maligne River. It wasn't too swift, but it was a little over waist deep at that time. Fortunately, it was early enough in the morning that there wasn't anyone else around. I took everything off from the waist down and put it up on my pack. I was going to wear my track shoes across the river but found out that the river bottom was very soft and silty, so I went with bare feet. I was glad I didn't need to get my track shoes wet. I got a stick to steady myself and put everything high on my pack and jacked my pack up as high on my shoulders as I could and started across. It worked out well, but needless to say, as I reached the other side everything from my navel down was quite numb. It only took a little while to get that warmed up because everything

What I called "Horse Crap Trail" coming into a meadow. If I lost the way, I would just follow the smell of the horse crap on the other side of the field.

else stayed pretty high and dry. After I dried my feet off and put my boots back on, I headed out again.

At about 10:00 that morning, I came across a bunch of young fellas in scout uniforms. I talked to them for a while about the trail and wished them well and took off again.

A little farther down the trail after I made it over the beautiful Maligne Pass, I saw a pretty lake that I hadn't expected to see. As I started down from the pass, I grew frustrated because the route was still a horse trail and not a very easy one for hikers. Every mile or two it would swing back across the stream, and not once was there a bridge for hikers. That meant there was no way for me to get across the river or its tributary streams without taking my boots off and putting them above my head as I hiked across

them. And quite a number of them were too wide and too swift to try skipping across the rocks. This process took time and effort, becoming quite an annoyance after a while. You would think they would have made some kind of provision for the hikers, too, but I guess they didn't feel it was that important, and I was certain that fording and re-fording the river wasn't a problem for the horses.

The creek that started at the top of Maligne Pass swelled quite rapidly as I descended. I counted the trail meandering back and forth across the same stream nine times before I finally got to a place where I made camp for that night. It had been a beautiful day, but I was getting a little perturbed by all those crossings. It reached the point where instead of putting my boots back on again, I just left my pants rolled up and my track shoes on

Columbia Ice Fields viewed from the Ice Fields Parkway.

I had left. My plan for the next morning was to take their exit to that Parkway and continue south on the highway. After wrenching my ankle, I was not in favor of staying back on the trail and hiking over more passes and fording more streams. That evening, I used the stream on my ankle and put it through one ice cycle, according to my athletic training class at the University of Montana. I then got a good night's sleep.

On August 7th, the next morning, I got up pretty early. I put my ankle through another ice cycle in the stream that morning. It then felt 100% better. After having some granola for breakfast and packing up, I took off for the Parkway. I got to the highway at mid-morning and talked to a few of the wardens there. I checked out of the trails and the forest and continued southeast on the road called the Icefields Parkway, which is the main artery between Jasper and Banff. Again, I hit this paved shoulder thing, but my legs and feet really felt good. Maybe it was the tire rubber on my boots.

I made it to a youth hostel, but it wasn't open until later that afternoon. I did meet the guy who ran it when I was having one of my own freeze-dried meals, and he gave me some tea. I thought I could make more distance, so after finishing my meal, I was on my way again.

It started to rain when I was about two miles short of the Columbia Ice Fields. I was pretty soaked by the time I rolled in there. They had a little tourist center, a restaurant, and so forth. Being wet, I was a bit chilly by the time I arrived. The gravitational winds coming off the glacier keep the area cool all year. I was able to get a good meal, which made up for being cold and wet.

and just kept right on walking. During my last ford, I hurried up a little bit too much across a really swift stream and ended up wrenching my ankle in between two big boulders as I went across. That mishap didn't do too much to help my mood.

The little campground where I stopped was at the trail junction at Poboktan Creek, and there was already a couple people camping there. They were a couple young fellas from back East who had just walked in from the Icefields Parkway, which was only about three miles away. It was really a nice little spot. And there was still enough daylight left to wash out a few socks and get those dry before the sun went down. I fixed myself a pretty good dinner from what

After dinner, I came out of the chalet-like building, and heard about a campground about a mile and a half down the road. I decided to spend the night there. As I made my way over, I met three people who were hitchhiking on the other side of the road. They were having no lucking getting a ride. One of them, Dick Martin, came across the road and asked me if I was just walking.

After my experience at Gita Creek, I no longer felt reluctant to tell people where I was going. I knew I wasn't crazy and I knew I wasn't going to fail to achieve my objective, so I started telling people exactly who I was and that I was walking from Alaska to Mexico.

I told that hitchhiker I had started in Hyder and was heading south to my goal. He was impressed and had many questions, so he ended up walking with me. The other two hitchhikers, Clark and Beth from California, came and joined us headed for the campground.

When we got there, we discovered that, like most of the campgrounds that time of year, it was filled. We tried to find one of the wardens to see if we could set up a couple tents somewhere out of the way. We ended up talking to a naturalist who seemed to be the only official in the area. He was about to start conducting what was called a campfire talk and invited us to join. We had hoped to get a place to camp, but instead sat through a two-hour lecture on the sex life of ferns. All four of us were really tired and didn't care too much about fern sex. Since no one appeared to be in charge, we went off into the woods, pitched our tents and crashed for the night without permission. It sprinkled for a while that night, but it was really no big deal.

Peaks near the Sunwapta Pass.

Camp kitchens were warm, dry shelters that saved us from having to pitch our tents. Photo courtesy of AlbertaWow.com.

The next morning, August 8th, was a bit chilly when we got up, which is always that way by the ice fields. That morning, I talked to Dick, and he said he wanted to walk with me to Banff, a distance of some 150 miles. I really appreciated the notion of having company for a while. We left Clark and Beth that morning and hiked over Sunwapta Pass. The highway in this particular area is just lined with wild strawberries. We didn't make a lot of miles, but we sure ate a lot of wonderful strawberries. We enjoyed each other's company and it was nice to have someone to share an adventure with. I started joking about him going all the way to Arizona with me. The mountain streams we went by were refreshing. We ended up camping that night next to the Alexander River on a little point that jetted out overlooking the river. We found a little clearing with a little patch of strawberries. We made a freeze-dried dinner and had a bunch of berries before we went to bed.

August 9th was another chilly morning. We headed out and walked about twelve miles to a little tourist trap called the Saskatchewan Crossing. On our way, we talked about all the little goodies we were going to buy once we got there. When we arrived, it was unbelievable. We had access to all sorts of good food; milk, ice cream, orange juice, peanut butter, cookies, you name it. It was very good, but it was also pretty expensive, probably because there were so many tourists there. When the busses arrived, we found ourselves in a long cafeteria line. It took us a while to get to our good food. As we were standing in line, Dick, just to be kind of comical, turned to this elderly lady behind him who'd just come off a tour bus and casually asked her if Nixon was still President. Now, I don't know why he thought about asking her this, but she said, "No, he resigned a few days ago." We were both pretty startled because we were in backwoods Canada, so it was the first we had heard about it.

Late that afternoon, we made it to a place called Waterfall Lakes Campground. The warden there was really nice, and he let us stay in the sheltered kitchen. That was really handy, saving us from having to mess with a tent. We just crashed on the tables, which worked out really well for camping. We also had a good dinner with some rice, sardines, and sweet rolls

that we'd picked up at the Saskatchewan Crossing.

The following morning, August 10th, we made the climb up and over Bow Pass, and it turned out to be quite a climb. Whether it was just that we were tired or whether it was actually that much of an incline, I don't know. We stopped close to the top and had some sandwiches and some fresh fruit that we had packed. It was really good to have some company, because Dick would carry the bread and the fresh fruit, which is weight you can really feel when you are climbing all day.

After we got over the pass, the rains came, but fortunately, there was a little place at Bow Lake with a sheltered kitchen. It was only about a 17-mile day, but since it didn't look like the rain was going to let up for a while, we just decided to spend the night there.

View fom the ice Fields Parkway north of Banff.

A guy and his family were already in the kitchen having dinner. They told us they were from Los Angeles originally, but were now living in Calgary, Alberta. The man had a fire pretty well stoked. Dick and I borrowed his axe and chopped enough firewood to keep the fire going for us all through night, with enough extra to stoke up another fire in the morning. The family left when they finished eating, leaving the kitchen and fire to us.

The rain let up for a little while, so Dick and I decided to get washed off a bit by taking a bath in the lake in our underwear. We got all warmed up by the fire and then ran into the lake and got soaped up, rinsed off, and ran back to the fire again. It was a refreshing way to get clean and, once we got warmed up again, we felt a lot better for having done it.

Later, we found out there was a lodge on Bow Lake. It started raining again, yet Dick and I were in dry clothes and were feeling pretty toasty by the fire. We decided it would be worth it to walk a couple miles back up and around Bow Lake to have a hot dinner at this lodge. The food was good, and we felt welcome, despite seeing a number of "Do Not" signs: Do not wear this, do not wear that, do not do this, do not do that. We joked about that with the waitress. When we had our fill, we then back through the rain to the sheltered kitchen and spent the night there.

The next morning, Sunday August 11th, we made a fire in the kitchen stove and ate a pretty good breakfast. We hiked approximately a 30-mile day all the way to Lake Louise. It was long enough of a workout that Dick's knee was beginning

View of from the Ice Fields Parkway of a house along the Bow River with the Canadian Rockies in the background.

to bother him. He told me that he had raced motorcycles in California for about six years and survived some crashes, one of which had quite a negative impact on his knee. We also discussed the impact of getting older. Dick was an old man of 29 years, and his birthday was December 23rd. I was 25, and my birthday is December 24th. We had a laugh about that coincidence.

When we reached Lake Louise, we planned to lay over the next day and just take it easy. We thought the distance to Lake Louise was going to be about 25 miles, but we underestimated the distance. Canada didn't have mile markers on the highways like we do in the U.S., so it was easy to judge it wrong. Thinking we would be there long before we were, the last five miles were pretty frustrating, especially since it started to rain. I was accustomed to this kind of thing, but it was new to Dick, and it didn't make it any easier that his knee was bothering him. Once we reached Lake Louise, his attitude was much more positive. Still he was glad we were going to take a day off.

We did not find any place to stay in the area for that evening, but we talked to people at a little hotel and made reservations there for the next night. It was quite reasonable price-wise—only $6.00 each. Needing someplace to stay in the meantime, we went down the road to a campground and were able to pitch our tent and stay for nothing. It rained all evening, but because we were looking forward to checking into the hotel the next morning, the rain didn't bother us too much.

The people at Lake Louise were extremely cordial and the service in the restaurant was excellent, with reasonable prices, as well. We were glad to be staying.

The next morning, we went back to the hotel where we had reservations and had breakfast before we checked into the room. Once there, we hung all of our wet gear up, got cleaned up and rested.

The hotel was right by the highway, not the lake, and with the rain, the whole mountain range was all socked in. While it might have been beautiful, the weather made us decide not to go up to Lake Louise. I was sure both of us would come back and see it sometime when the weather was nicer. Instead, we enjoyed a very dry, cozy, and restful day inside.

After that great day of rest, we took off again on August 13th. We had a hearty breakfast at the local café before we hit the road around 9:00 a.m.

We got on Highway 1A, which is the old highway from Lake Louise to Banff. The traffic on the old road was a lot less, and there was a good gravel shoulder to walk on. After a pleasant start, we stopped at a place called Baker Creek, had lunch, and continued the rest of the day walking.

We stopped for the night at a place called Eisenhower Junction adjacent to Mount Eisenhower. We camped in another sheltered kitchen, eating a little of our own food before we went to the fine local restaurant and finished dinner with apple pie à la mode for dessert. That night, it rained hard, but we were still dry with that roof over our heads.

The next morning, August 14th, was chilly, I guess due to the elevation. The weather stayed a little damp. We left our packs in the camp kitchen and went back to the restaurant at the junction for a hot breakfast and to get warmed up.

After returning for our packs, we continued on the old highway headed for Banff. About four miles out, the old road finally joined the main highway. The previous day's rest had been good for Dick's knee. My own ankles had recovered from wrenching them the previous week fording all those rivers. It was only about 20 miles from the Castle Junction to Banff, and we did the first four in one hour, despite a light rain. What a great start! We didn't have a long hike planned, so we slowed down a little bit as the day progressed.

We stopped to rest at Johnston Canyon just as a couple tour busses pulled up. We were sitting on the steps outside the restaurant and curio shop, looking pretty shabby with our beards and fairly long hair, having milk and cookies in the rain. One of the busses was filled with elderly folks. One elderly guy came out of the door of the store complaining because he had lost his wife. Right behind him was another grey-haired gentleman who said with a very British accent, "You are a lucky fellow." We all had a chuckle.

As we took off again, we ran across a great big chain of wild raspberry bushes right alongside the highway. We stopped for a few of them and then hurried to Banff.

In Banff, we stopped at the King Edward Hotel, but they were filled up for that night. They called around town for us and discovered that the only spaces available were private residences that took people in and charged a few bucks. We made reservations at the King Edward Hotel for the following night and they arranged for us to stay with the Fisk family that night. They gave us the address and told us how to get there. We found it and had a good evening with the Fisks after dinner.

Kananaski River.

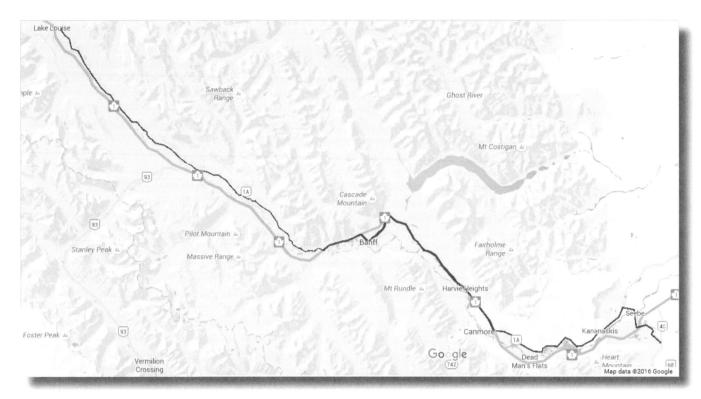

The next morning, August 15th, we left our packs at the Fisk's house and had a good time playing tourist for a little while before checking in to the King Edward Hotel in time for a good breakfast. After that, we went back to the Fisk's house, got our packs, and did some of our laundry.

Banff was a lot like Jasper in many ways, so we had fun there. We checked out most of the sporting goods stores in the area, as Dick was looking for another pair of boots. He wasn't sure then if he was going to continue walking with me or hitchhike directly back home to Jerome, Arizona from Banff. I was pretty sure he'd hitchhike from Banff, but he seemed a little reluctant that day to make a firm decision.

On August 16th, we went to Smitty's for breakfast, and I had one of my favorites: Strawberry waffles. Later that day, we saw an old train from the last century parked in the Banff train

yard and took a guided tour of it. Dick said he had been kind of a train freak as a kid. He told me a lot of his train stories as we toured the train's club cars and dining cars, decorated with pictures from the late 1800s. It was a little sad, because I was pretty sure I was going to be losing Dick's good company. I was going to miss his friendship.

That afternoon, I began readying myself for the next morning and the next leg of the trip, buying groceries

90

and getting all my gear squared away. That evening, we caught a Chinese dinner and after dinner went to the movie *American Graffiti*. It was the second time each one of us had seen it, but we both enjoyed it very much. We had ice cream cones after the flick and headed back to the hotel and went to bed.

On August 17th, we got up at about 6:00 a.m. and checked out of the hotel early. Then we caught breakfast again at Smitty's, and after breakfast, we parted company. Dick headed for the Trans-Canada to hitch a ride south, and I walked on a little shortcut that I had seen on the map. I was alone again.

I got out to the Trans-Canada eventually, and at about 9:30 that morning, a truck pulled up. Just as I was about to give the driver my "appreciate the offer" spiel, Dick jumped out the other side. He got his pack out of the back and walked with me again for a little

while. We got to a place not far up the road called Carrot Creek. It was a very nice day, so I changed into my shorts, said goodbye agaidn and took off. I left him sitting on the bridge at Carrot Creek with his thumb out. I told him that I would look him up if I came anywhere near Jerome while I was heading through Arizona.

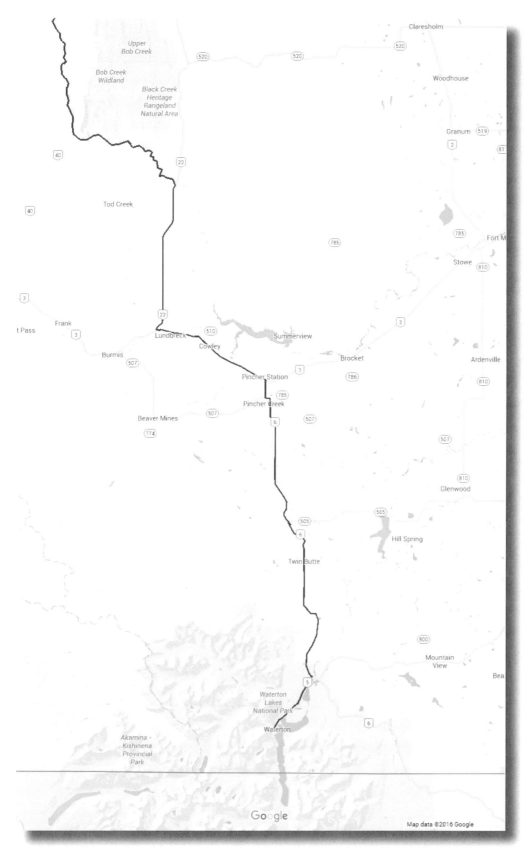

Then I was alone again really this time. A few miles down the road, I emerged from Banff National Park. I went through a gate and got on highway 1A again, the old highway, and followed that to the Bow Valley Provincial Campground just short of the little town of Seebee.

I stayed there that evening and was able to get a shower and fixed myself a nice meal out of my pack, ending a mostly sunny, mellow day.

I fell asleep comfortable in the sheltered kitchen, but was awoken around 3:00 a.m. by a munching sound coming from inside my backpack. What the heck? I got up, grabbed my flashlight, and shined it down in my pack. There was a mouse just about to get into my peanut butter container. It had nibbled on a number of things already and was awfully chubby. I dumped it out of the pack, and it waddled off. It was the first wild animal encounter I had in quite some time.

When I got up later that morning, I gave my brother Kevin a call and made sure everything was okay there in Missoula. It was great to hear his voice and talk to him for a while. He let me know that he and Mom were doing well.

After hanging up, I walked down the highway for a couple miles until I came to a road called the Kananaskis. It was a dirt road named after the river and lake nearby that paralleled the Continental Divide. I and my legs looked forward to being off the pavement for a good stretch.

Fortunately it was Sunday, so the construction that was taking place on the northernmost part of the road wasn't very active. Quite a few local people were on the road, weekending up at the Kananaskis Lake and River. I was able to make about a 27-mile day.

I arrived at a campground that was populated with campers from Calgary and Saskatoon. Several families having a picnic were kind enough to invite me over for a burger, hot dog, and potato salad. I had a nice time talking to them.

Because I had seen a black bear on the road that day, and there was a bunch of garbage around the camp, I was concerned about our safety. When I found a spot for the night in the sheltered kitchen, I put my pack up in the rafters so as not to attract bears. Plenty of daylight was still left, so I ended up taking a bath in the river. It was a bit nippy, which made it pretty refreshing, and it felt good to get clean again. That evening, I went to

sleep on the floor of the sheltered kitchen. The bears were no problem, but a mouse was running around the kitchen that kept buzzing my head and getting in my hair. Frustrated, I hopped up on a table and slept there for the rest of the night.

I got up very early the next morning, August 19th, and I knew from looking at the map that I had a long day ahead of me. I had to go over the Highwood Pass to Highwood Junction, my destination for that day. With a 45-mile day ahead, I got going when it was still dark, fixed some granola in my water and dried milk, and was on the road by 6:30 a.m.

The morning was chilly, so I put on my rain pants to give me some relief from the cold. I made pretty good time that morning because I didn't stop for anything. I made it to Highwood Summit by about noon that day, and I ate lunch there. The sign said the summit was 7,200 feet high.

A little later, as I was going down the other side of the pass, I got caught in a bad rainstorm that poured on me for about three hours. I was soaking wet and in the middle of nowhere when a car filled with Native Americans stopped to pick me up. When I explained to them that I was just walking, they couldn't believe me, but they wished me luck.

I finally reached the Junction at about 8:30 that evening. The sign on door of little store said that they had just closed at 8:00, a half hour before I got there. Fortunately, the lady inside who ran the place was kind enough to let me in and make me a couple sandwiches. It was kind of a hunting lodge and restaurant type place, and I was able to rent a hunting cabin for the evening and get my stuff hung up and dried out. When I went to bed, I slept extremely well because I was very tired. I Before I went to sleep, I marked the end of my second month on the road.

My two-month milestone marked a second event in my life. The next day, August 20th, was six years since I had enlisted in the Navy. This was also officially my Discharge Day. I had signed up for a four year enlistment, to which the Navy adds two years inactive reserve when they had the right to simply call me back. As of this day, my commitment to the Navy was completely finished and I truly felt discharged. I had done my duty and then some. I loved being on the SEAL Teams. Even though I came back to a country that was relentlessly negative to military veterans like me, on this day, I only felt a sense of satisfaction.

When I left the Teams to go to college, it was very much my plan to return to the SEALs as an officer. I loved the brotherhood and the challenge. The executive officer of SEAL Team TWO, LT Davis, highly recommended that I be allowed to return to the command as an officer when I finished my degree. Now, well into my walk, and especially after my insight in Gita Creek, I made a firm decision not to return to the SEALs.

It is funny to think of such a demanding job as being a refuge and place of comfort, but for me it was. I knew God had other plans for me. I felt cared for, protected and approved of out here in the mountains all by myself. I knew I would carry that with me no matter where I went. I didn't have to go back to a safe place. On this day, alone again after leaving Dick on the side of the road, I began to seriously think about what was next for me after I crossed the border into Mexico. I turned my walking meditations to this topic.

Since I had made so many miles the previous day, I could take it a little easier. I got started at about 9:30 a.m. and had been on the road for a couple hours when it warmed up pretty well. The sun was shining, so I changed into my shorts. There was another pass to go over, but it was not very high, only an elevation of about 6,800 feet. At the summit, I met some folks in a pickup with a camper. They offered me a ride, and I thanked them and let them know that I was just walking. They were very nice people, headed for the same place I was, the Livingston Campground.

When I rolled in about 5:45 p.m., they were already there. I went over and talked with them for a while. They were the Kehrs, Max, Betty, and their two boys, from Vulcan, Alberta where they had a farm on the prairie. We chatted for quite a while, and Betty fixed me dinner that night. Their two sons asked me all kinds of questions about my trip because they were very interested. I felt I could be me, no longer guarding or concealing parts of my story. I told them the works, about being a SEAL, being a Vietnam vet and about walking from Alaska to Mexico. I didn't care if they judged me, and they didn't do so. After dinner, they went to bed in their camper, and I went onto a table in the sheltered kitchen. We were all out of the rain that night.

On the morning of August 21st, I fixed breakfast and took off in the sunshine at about 8:30 a.m. About ten miles down the dirt road, I stopped for coffee with some fish and wildlife wardens. I had met one of these guys on the road the day before. They were conducting some kind of a survey out there, a research project on

Prince of Wales Hotel in Waterton, Alberta.

fish or something. I'm not sure what their deal was, but they did give me a few cups of coffee, and I got to talk a while with the three or four guys who were there. Their trailer was on Dutch Creek.

Down the road, I headed for a shortcut that was going to cut a couple miles off my day. That meant having to ford another river, which wasn't a very big deal, despite stubbing my toe. It was a shortcut, so that was fortunate.

I emerged from the dirt road back on a paved road close to the Oldman River, which cuts through the mountains at a place called The Gap. As I came down from the mountains of the Continental Divide range through The Gap, suddenly there before me was just flat prairie stretching as far as I could see to the east.

I followed the Oldman River to a campground near Maycroft, Alberta on that prairie. In those few miles there was a big change. I could look back west at the mountains, and I could look east that was just flat as a table top. I had been getting pretty spoiled because I hadn't had to fool with my tent for quite a number of nights, enjoying the warm, dry protection of camp kitchen tables. This night was no exception. While I was settling in late that afternoon, I met an elderly gentleman who had been there for a couple of days fishing, and he was really a nice fellow.

The next morning, August 22nd, the fisherman I had talked with the night before came over early at 6:00 a.m. as the sun was just coming up, with three eggs for breakfast, which I fixed quickly. We then chatted for a while as I was packing up and putting my hiking boots on. He complimented me on the hike that I was doing, and he said he'd never seen anything like that before.

By this time, I was well onto the prairie, which reminded me a lot of eastern Montana. My mom was born and raised just outside of Flaxville, where her parents homesteaded in the northeast corner of Montana, close to the Canadian border. I've got a couple uncles, Irvin and Johnny, who are still farming and ranching out there.

As I pounded out the miles, I found the people were extremely friendly here. Quite a number of them stopped and, and they seemed to be interested in what I was doing. That afternoon it got pretty hot because there were no clouds in the sky at all and no shadows anywhere.

I reached the little town of Lundbreck at about 1:30 that afternoon. Unfortunately the town had no restaurant, but there was a tavern that a lady told me was open. So I went over to see what they had to eat and ended up getting one of those ready-made pizzas. I met a couple of really nice people there by the name of Kate and Stan Warriner. They were ranchers in the area, and Stan had just broken his leg from a horse riding fall. We had a nice talk, and they bought me a couple of 7-Ups.

Shortly thereafter, I left Lundbreck and stopped at a little town down the road called Cowley and got some ice cream and milk. That satisfied a few of my cravings. I stayed that night at another sheltered kitchen on the Castle River, where I met another couple who were already there. They were really a couple of fine characters; two folks in their mid- to late-fifties. He called her Vivian, and she called him Johnny Boy. He had a funny hat on, not a tooth in his head, and wore two shirts. Vivian was a rather short woman with white hair long enough in front that it kept falling down in her eyes. She often tried to pin it back without much success. I wanted very much to get a picture of them, but he didn't want me to do that.

Johnny Boy did most of the talking, and it was about the Depression and World War I. That evening when we all turned in, they went to bed on their picnic table, and I went to bed on mine. I guessed that he was waiting to meet somebody or something, because he kept getting up through the night and checking the fire and looking all around, and then he'd go back to sleep for an hour or so.

I woke up on the morning of August 23rd, had some breakfast and said goodbye to Johnny Boy and Vivian. I was glad to be in for a very easy day after a restless night. I was only going to go as far as the town of Pincher Creek, about seven miles away. I had another breakfast at the Pincher Station truck stop before I walked a few miles more to Pincher Creek and checked into a room. I bought some supplies, got a good rest, and even got to watch some television, which I hadn't seen in quite some time. It's funny how much you can appreciate little things like that after being without them for quite a while.

On August 24th, I slept in a bit and was on the road after a big breakfast about 10:15 a.m. I only made about 17 miles that day and decided I'd give my feet and ankles a bit more rest. I found another sheltered kitchen that afternoon at Yarrow Creek, which was a good reason to stop where I did. After dinner, I spent the night on another picnic table. Fortunately, this one was a little larger than some of them had been at other shelters. I needed the rest because I was planning to push pretty hard the next few days. I was so close to the U.S. border. I was looking forward to getting to Waterton and Glacier National Park, known as the International Peace Park, on the U.S./Canadian border. My goal was to get as far as the town of Waterton the following day.

On Sunday morning, about 7:30 a.m. on August 25th, I left Yarrow Creek. I was able to call home from the little town of Twin Butte. I made it to the town of Waterton that afternoon because it was only 17 miles away. I was really happy. Growing up in KaIispell, Montana, I had been there about a half dozen times as a tourist. It was great to see this beautiful, familiar country again.

That afternoon, I got a hotel room and looked forward to being able to have another very relaxing evening. I went out after checking in and played tourist that afternoon. I stopped at the information center and got some maps of the Waterton and Glacier Park trails. I found a trail that went from the town of Waterton due south on the west shore of Waterton Lake which straddles the U.S./Canada border. The trail then came back into the U.S. and then went to Goat Haunt in Glacier Park at the southern tip of the lake. I was very glad to see on the maps that hiking on the trails in both parks was quite a few miles less than it would have been to stay on the highways, which brightened up the afternoon quite a bit. The cozy Waterton hotel where I found my room was a log building with a big fireplace in the lobby. My room was very clean and comfortable. I celebrated that with a wonderful dinner and two double huckleberry ice cream cones.

CHAPTER 5
Returning to Montana

On the morning of August 26th, I ate breakfast in the hotel and then took off as the sun came up. I headed south on the Boundary Trail on the western border of Waterton Lake. According to the map, the U.S. border was only 5 miles away, and I was extremely elated about that. I had been away from home more than two months and crossing back into the U.S., especially so close to where I grew up, was both an accomplishment and a homecoming. To be someplace familiar, and soon to be with family and friends, heartened me more than I expected.

I went through customs at a place called Goat Haunt, about five miles into the States at the southern end of the lake. It wasn't that big a deal really. I talked with the customs officer there and the ranger. They asked me what I had in my pack, and I explained that all I had brought back to the U.S. was about $30 worth of freeze-dried food. We didn't have to take everything out and weed through it, which was fortunate. I made arrangements with the ranger to get me booked into a place called the 50 Mountain Campground for that evening.

Sunset in Glacier Park, Montana.

As I left Goat Haunt, I started climbing a trail that went straight up. It was good to be back on mountain trails in Glacier Park. There was not a cloud in the sky, and the hiking temperature was comfortable. As my trail climbed up to the Continental Divide where the 50 Mountain Campground was located, the greater the view became of all the Waterton and Glacier mountains and valleys.

I reached the campground a couple hours before dark. I met a German gentleman Gerhart Henshel. I talked with him quite a bit, and we found we were on similar missions. He was on a exploration trip, traveling all over the country in a pickup truck and a camper. He loved hiking in Glacier Park, so here he was. He lived in Salt Lake City and worked as an engineer at the Snowbird Ski Resort in Utah.

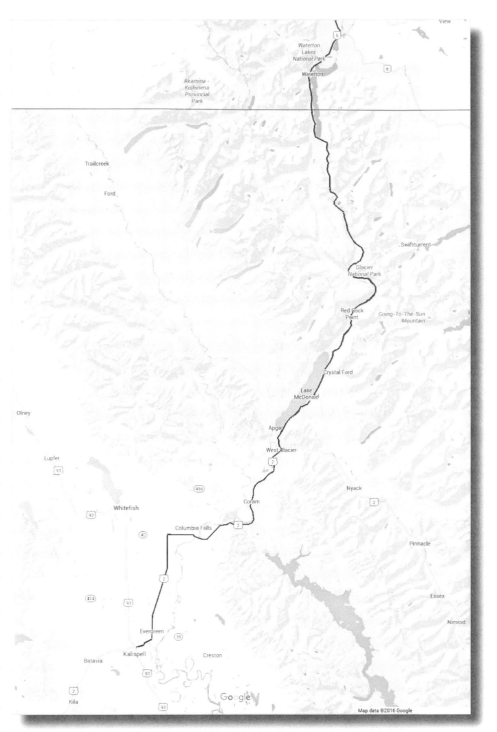

The sunset that evening was fantastic, as if the whole sky was on fire. They call this place 50 Mountain because from here, you can see 50 different mountain peaks in the area of the Continental Divide. The moment was all the more magical when a doe and a couple of fawns came near the cabin. Apparently people fed them and didn't give them any trouble, so they were tame. I arrived pretty sweaty from the climb, and the doe came up and licked the salt off my hands. It was really neat.

Nearly tame deer greeted me at the 50 Mountain Campground.

I was invited to sleep that evening on the floor of the shelter cabin, not in the campground, which assured I got a very good night's sleep. It was just on a concrete floor, but with my sleeping pad, a roof over my head, and not having to worry about grizzly bears, it was very restful.

The next morning of August 27th, I got started about 8:00 a.m. after saying goodbye to Gerhart. I definitely planned to look him up when I got near Salt Lake City. It was a beautiful day, and he was heading toward Granite Park on the Highline Trail. Just as we were parting company, I gave him the address of my aunt and uncle in the Flathead Valley and my mom and brother in Missoula. If it was necessary, they would give him a place to

stay for a while. We said goodbye, and I headed down the trail.

I figured it would be kind of a downhill grade that day, and it was to begin with. The morning was frustrating because the Flattop Mountain Trail wasn't very well-marked. It kept doubling back on itself, and I kept losing track of the markers. When I would reach a meadow, the trail would fan out and become indistinguishable, and it'd take me a while to find the trail again on the other side of the meadow.

I was told to watch out for grizzly bears. I saw a number of signs of them being nearby. I didn't have a weapon with me, but I did have bells on my pack to let them know I was coming and give them a chance to run off. The trail wove through a bunch of thimbleberries and huckleberries. Since they were in season, the bushes were heavy with them. I just ate and ate and ate huckleberries and thimbleberries by the double handfuls. They were delicious, and I knew that the bears loved them, too.

Suicidal thoughts are one of the symptoms of PTSD, but I didn't suffer from them. And now, well into my hike, my mindset was one of feeling spiritually connected and protected. I watched out for grizzlies, but I did not fear them. We got shot at so much in Vietnam, we all got a bit fatalistic. In combat, you get to the point where you say to yourself, "If I get killed, then I get killed." The one thing we couldn't stand was the thought of losing a Teammate. Since I was alone, I had only myself to worry about. As a result, I figured that if I was supposed to be lunch for a grizzly, so be it. They chose to leave me alone and I loved them for that.

The trail itself finally emerged out onto the road just below what they

A mountain lake in Glacier Park I passed along my walk.

called "The Switchback" (now renamed "The Loop") on the Going-to-the-Sun Highway. The scenery on this road is spectacular. McDonald Creek flows right beside it. I stopped and had a little lunch by this stream and was just enjoying the day, the trip, the people, and the surroundings. I stopped when I got to the Lake McDonald Lodge and caught some dinner, with some milk and Hostess Cup Cakes for dessert. I also chatted with a few of the tourists before I started down the road again and got a few more miles in before dark.

It was such a mild evening that I just put my sleeping pad and sleeping bag out and slept there in the bushes by the side of the road next to the lake. It was a little bit before sunset, so I stripped down and took a swim. Since the lake is glacier-fed, it stays pretty chilly year-round, making for a very refreshing swim. "Training is not over" ran through my mind. SEAL training always involves lots of cold.

On the morning of August 28th, I got an early start after my granola breakfast at about 7:00 a.m. By the time I reached West Glacier, I was hungry again, so I had another breakfast at the café there.

As I was getting packed up after that breakfast, I ran into Pete Vogel and Jack Steinhorst, the guys whom I had met just outside of Vanderhoof British Columbia riding their bicycles. They, of course, had taken a much wider sweep of the countryside to get there than I did and were stopping more frequently. It was really good to see them again.

My spirits were very high hiking in this particular area. Growing up in Kalispell, we enjoyed spending a good deal of time in Glacier Park. It was just like being home again. I was very familiar with the country and was really enjoying the walk.

At about 3:00 p.m., I arrived at the little town of Hungry Horse. There was a couple there by the name of Marv and Roz whose daughter Darlene I had dated for a while at the University of Montana. These folks still owned the Hungry Horse Motel. I meant to just pop in and say "hello," and visit with them for a while, but they invited me to stay that night. Thank Goodness! That afternoon, I spent most of my time swimming in their motel pool, relaxing in the room they gave me, and talking with them. That evening, they fed me extremely well; we had a steak dinner and just a nice mellow evening. Their two sons were still at home then, so I got to see them again, too. Unfortunately, Darlene wasn't there. I had an amazing night's rest because I hadn't been in a real bed for quite some time.

On August 29th, Roz made me a tremendous breakfast and piled on the pancakes. Wow! I then said goodbye to them in Hungry Horse, not a bit hungry, and headed for my Norwegian aunt and uncle's farm (the Lorentzens) that was about twelve miles down the road. I began what was going to be a short and very pleasant sunny and beautiful day.

I headed through Bad Rock Canyon on Highway 2, then through Columbia Heights, and remained on the highway due south of there. I reached the farm about 2:00 p.m. As I turned east down Small's Lane, the road that leads to the farm, I ran into my Uncle Chjald, which is Norwegian for Charles and is pronounced "shawl" and Cousin Ivan, the guy who took Buzz and me to Seattle.

It was really great to see them and fun to be back home in the Flathead Valley. My mom, dad, younger brother, and I lived in a number of different homes in Kalispell, Montana, about ten miles from the farm, and I, myself, did a lot of growing up there on that property. If I can call any one place home, this farm is it.

Walking up the lane, I thanked God for helping me to get there! It wasn't just the walk, avoiding bears and not getting hit by a truck. It was getting through Vietnam safely and getting to a better place emotionally during the walk. My feeling of gratitude was for everything.

When I made it to the farmhouse, my aunt and grandmother (my mom's mom) were as glad to see me as I was to see them. Being with family members again really warmed me up. They were amazed, as well, knowing that I had walked there from Chuck's home in Alaska.

Later that afternoon, Ivan took me into Kalispell to a shoe repair shop to get my boots resoled again. Driving into town at the speed limit to me felt like we were going 100 miles per hour after traveling at three miles per hour for over two months. Ivan and I both got a kick out of that.

After we dropped my boots off, Ivan and his wife Connie (with whom I had gone to school) invited me to stay with them in town for the Labor Day weekend. Wow! I loved being able to spend that much time with them, and we had a wonderful evening together that night. They shared with me where they were working and how they felt about it. I then answered some of their questions about my current hike.

The following day, I spent time with some of my friends with whom I had grown up in Kalispell and hadn't seen in a long time. Jim Leary was the first

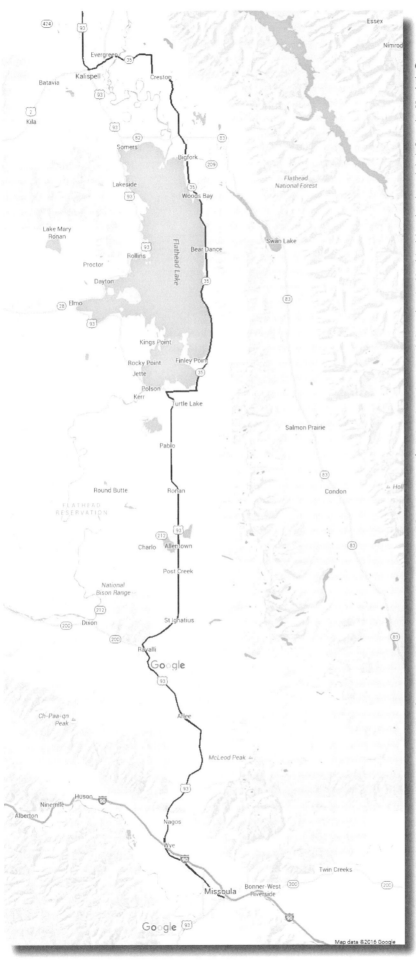

call I made. He and his wife Bonnie had spent the summer in town since he had left active duty in the U.S. Navy. We had played Little League baseball together (my dad was the coach) and remained very close friends through high school and after. I was the best man at their wedding in 1971, right after I returned from Vietnam. Fortunately, I was able to get together with him and his family that afternoon. Jim's father, John Leary, was one of Carlson's Raiders in the U.S.M.C. during World War II in the South Pacific. Because he was one of my World War II combat heroes the entire time I was growing up and had filled the role of father after my dad died, it was great to see him again, too. Jim's mother, Phyllis, was one of my extra mothers, as well. We had a wonderful visit that afternoon, and they asked me a lot about how I got here from Alaska.

Labor Day weekend in Kalispell is a big holiday. The

community has a big golf tournament, and the holiday itself is a good excuse for a lot of people to come back to the Flathead Valley. I reconnected with Pete and Beth Wilkey, the people I stayed with in Spokane on our way through Seattle to Alaska. The guy I worked for at the spa in Missoula, Doug Bitney, was also there with his wife, Nancy. One evening that weekend, we all went to a party given by Linda Simpson, a girl we all grew up with and her husband.

To say the least, my homecoming from the hike was far different from my Vietnam homecoming. I had forged a new identity on my hike to go along with my newfound sense of peace. No longer was I the crazy Vietnam vet. Instead I was that admirably crazy guy who had just walked from Alaska.

I saw people I hadn't seen in years. We had some nice talks, and it was great to hear about where they were and what they were doing. Many of them were also curious about my trip, my military service experience, about the places I'd been, and the things that I'd seen. I felt totally comfortable talking about everything and didn't feel the need to carefully edit my responses like I did before I left on the hike. They last time these people saw me, I had a Navy haircut and was pretty squared away. Now, here I was in the same worn clothes that I had lived in for three months, and I had a beard and long hair. Some of them thought that was pretty funny.

I spent most of September 1st with Ivan, Connie, and the rest of my Lorentzen family. I happy to get my resoled boots back; thankful they got them done before the holiday kicked in. Back to the farm that afternoon, we all had a wonderful dinner, which was typical. I also felt lucky to get another great night's sleep.

On September 2nd, I woke up early. My Aunt Agnes fixed a breakfast that was unbelievable. She also took a picture of me with my pack on just before I headed out. I waddled out of the farm fully stuffed and took off for the highway at about 7:45 a.m. The four days' rest and spending time with all those amazing folks had done me a world of good. I got off to a fine start.

My aunt Agnes took this picture of me before I left the farm to head to Missoula.

I headed south to the east shore of Flathead Lake. I knew that it was only going to take me four days to get to Missoula, so I enjoyed a moderate pace. Traveling by foot, I was really able to appreciate my surroundings. I thought back to all those miles through Canada, remembering specific sights, sounds, smells and feelings. I listened to the sound of the wind in the trees, the flow of the river beside the road. I marveled that late in the summer, it flowed slowly and seems to slide into the shadows under the trees. I turned my gaze to the golden light of the sun on the mountains. Besides the steady crunch of my feet on the gravel alongside the road, I heard the gorgeous song of the birds. I felt gifted and gave thanks for the time to leisurely make my way through this beautiful world up close.

I met Paul Driscoll, one of the bicyclists I had met in Canada, just south of Bigfork. He was going south back home to Jackson Hole, Wyoming. Paul was having a few problems with his bike, but hoped he could hold it together until he got to Missoula. I gave him the name of a good bike shop there where I was sure he could get it fixed. When we parted company, I headed south.

It wasn't too long, just a few miles down the road, when Paul on his bicycle came zinging by me after he'd eaten lunch. A couple of hours after that, I heard somebody yelling at me from the bushes beside a lake. There on the other side of the road was Paul. He had parked his bike and was going for a swim. We wished each other well, and I continued walking. After Paul dried off, he packed up and passed me again. It wasn't too far down the road before I ran into him for the last time that day. There he was, forlorn on the side of the road, thumb in the air. The rear wheel of his bike had finally given out, so he needed a ride to Missoula. I gave him my mom and brother's address, so he would have a place to stay while he was getting his bike fixed. He said that now he felt he and I were like the tortoise and the hare: he kept passing me up, and I kept catching up to him. Paul did end up staying with Mom and Kevin in Missoula, waiting to get his bike fixed so he could get back to his home in Jackson Hole safely.

I wound up spending the night at a little campground at Yellow Bay. The campground itself was closed, but I talked with the people taking care of the place. They said that since there was no one else in the campground, I was just walking and was much too tired to go any farther, that I could pitch my tent in the campground that evening. It was such a nice evening that I picked a thick group of trees for shelter and didn't

have to pitch my tent. I woke up in the middle of the night, and the moonlight was shining down through the branches. It was a balmy evening and so beautiful. I did get a good night's rest.

I was up at 7:30 a.m. on the morning of September 3rd to a granola breakfast. I set off for Polson, Montana some 18 miles away at the southern end of Flathead Lake. I pigged out on a burger and fries at a local drive-in right there on the highway. I continued on to the little town of Ronan.

This little town was a very important stop for me. I made a bee line to Don Aadsen Ford. Don had been a good friend of my late dad's in Kalispell. They had met over business, as my dad

Sunrise over the Mission Mountains south of Ronan, Montana.

106

had a collection agency that worked with Don's Ford dealership. Seeing Don was as close as I could get to seeing my dad. Don had followed my achievements through life. He was a fan of the Kalispell Lions, the team I played on and that my dad coached. Don had daughters, so I was something like the son he never had. He followed my SEAL training. I called my dad every week telling him about Hell Week, drown-proofing and other challenges. Then my dad would call Don. They both shared pride in what I was doing. He told me that my dad would have been very proud of me making this walk. He told me that he himself sure was and that he wished he could do something similar. It did me a world of good talking to Don.

Don gave me some advice about where to camp. I ended up spending the night in the Ronan City Park, again in another shelter kitchen on a picnic table. And before I went to sleep, I was able to have dinner at the nearby Dairy Queen.

The next morning, September 4th, I got up and had some breakfast in Ronan and took off. It was a cloudy morning in the beautiful Mission Valley with the amazing Mission Mountains off to my left. Even though it wasn't sunny, it was a very beautiful day, and I took a few pictures of the mountain range. I had made the trip between Kalispell and Missoula many times, but always in a car. It's funny how much more I noticed when I was walking.

A little later on in the morning, I talked to a farmer who was fixing his fence next to the road. He told me about his crops and the weather. I guess the Mission Valley had had bumper crops that year. Walking had another benefit: Besides noticing all the details, I enjoyed the chance to strike up conversations with people along the way.

Just before a got to Ravalli Hill, my friend John Leary stopped and chatted with me for a while. He was heading south on a trip to Missoula. He said he'd catch me on the way back later in the afternoon. When I got to the other side of Ravalli Hill, I stopped and had lunch. My route took me through the Flathead Indian Reservation, adjacent to one of the largest buffalo ranges in the United States.

A little farther down the road south of the town of Ravalli, I stopped in Spring Creek at the beginning of the Jocko Valley. After I pulled over and put my pack down, I took my shirt off and dunked a bit in the creek. When I was back on the highway, John Leary happened by again, heading back north towards Kalispell. We both enjoyed another chat. Afterward he wished me luck, said he was proud of me, and headed back to his home.

I continued south to the Willow Creek Campground by the Jocko River, just north of Arlee, Montana. The guy who owned it was a young carpenter. He told me the normal fee there was two dollars. People on 10-speed bikes pay one dollar, but walkers don't have to pay anything. He said he wasn't losing too much money on that deal. I thanked him very much and spent a nice comfortable night there just outside Arlee.

On September 5th, I got up early that morning and was on the road by about 7:30 a.m.. At about 8:00 a.m. a truck came by me just north of Arlee, and I thought I recognized the driver. A few minutes later, the truck turned around and came back. I was right—I did know the driver. He was Jim Cordial, the father of a really good friend of mine in Missoula. Jim stopped and I told him about my trip. He wished me well before continuing north to Polson.

Three or four miles south of the town of Arlee, I saw a few young ladies who were bicycling to Missoula, returning from a trip up to Flathead Lake. We talked for a while and shared some details regarding both of our trips. One of them was Debbie, a journalist at the *Missoulian* newspaper.

After we parted, I continued on to the junction of Highway 93 and Interstate 90. At the truck stop there, I stopped in to see Lenard Legried, the owner of a Peterbilt Truck dealership. Leonard and I were good friends from before I started my hike because he used to come into the spa where I worked to exercise frequently.

He had a lot of questions about my hike, and after he took a picture of me with my pack in front of one of his trucks, he took me next door to the restaurant and bought me lunch.

Next I headed into town down the north side of the Interstate. It was only about eight more miles to Missoula. About two or three miles down the road, a four-wheel drive vehicle pulled off in front of me. The driver jumped out and started taking pictures of me. I didn't know what was going on until he explained to me that he was Harley Hettick, a photographer for the *Missoulian*. He said Jim Cordial called them a little earlier and let them know that a guy was walking into town that day from Alaska. We talked for a while, and he told me to get in touch with the *Missoulian* when

I got into town and gave me the name of the guy to ask for. As we parted company, I thanked him, and he wished me well.

A couple more miles down the road, a gal by the name of Gyla happened to drive by and stopped nearby with her two little kids, Brent and Stephanie, in the back seat. I had dated her for a while before I took off for Alaska. I walked up to the car and put my head in the window. Stephanie, who was about 18 months old and only knew a few words, looked at me, looked at her mom, got kind of a puzzled look on her face, pointed at me, and just said "bear." It was really funny and something that Gyla wouldn't let me forget. She gave me some water and cookies.

Me at my brother's wedding to his bride Jeannie with my mother Cecelia.

108

The Hiker

September 15, 1974
Missoulian

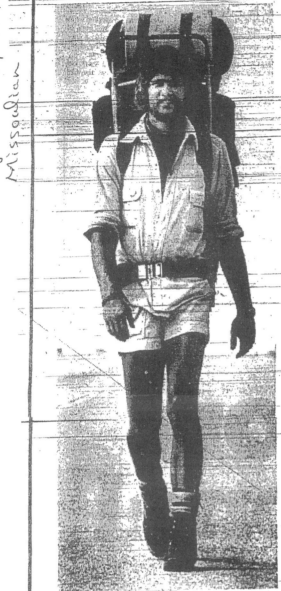

followed a portion of the divide trail to the Columbia Ice Fields. He then proceeded to Banff, south to Glacier National Park and finally home to Missoula.

The six-foot-five hiker walked alone most of the way. He started the trip with Buzz Blastic, a Missoula high school teacher, but Blastic, having obligations at home and school, could only accompany Burham the first 100 miles.

A second traveling companion, Dick Martin from Arizona, hiked another 100-mile stretch.

"I don't feel any great problem being alone. You've got a lot of time to think things out," he said. But it is nice to have someone to walk with. They see things you don't and can share them with you, Burham added.

Burham has taken only one ride, but receives between three and six offers each day. He had to accept the ride early in his trek when his first pair of boots fell apart and his feet got infected. He got a lift to the nearest town, 50 miles away. When his feet healed he hitchhiked back to the spot where he accepted the ride and made up the mileage.

Mosquitoes and flies have been the bane of his hike. "The bugs are horrendous. The weather you can become used to. You learn not to fight the elements, but never did I get used to the bugs," he said.

Food and shelter have been adequate. With travelers checks as currency, he said he picks up food "wherever I can get it," planning in 200-mile sections at a time.

As for shelter, Burham sleeps wherever he happens to be. He has stayed with farmers, in campgrounds, alongside the road — you name it. Even an occasional hotel. "I treat myself," he said.

"Things you take for granted you can really come to appreciate after not having them," commented Burham.

Reactions to the hike have been varied. "You run into a certain percentage of people that don't want to have anything to do with you," he said. But the majority have been great. "They've taken me into their homes, fed me, given me a place to sleep."

"Hikers or anybody who travels under their own steam are really appreciative of what you're doing," he said.

"I've seen a lot of really beautiful country, but the high point has been the people, the opportunity to meet them. I've really met some characters," he said.

Burham plans to return to Missoula to finish school after the hike. He said he is keeping a fairly accurate journal and hopes to "put something together" in way of a book to share his experiences. Other than that "it's awfully hard to tell," he said.

By DEBBIE McKINNEY

On June 19, 25-year-old Greg Burham left Hyder, Alaska, with the intention of walking to Mexico.

Now, three months and three pairs of boots later, Burham has walked almost 1,400 miles and some of his acquaintances are still "writing me off as crazy," he said.

Carrying a pack ranging from 60 to 80 pounds and walking 25 to 30 miles a day, Burham, a Missoula resident, arrived here last week to meet his only deadline the Sept. 14 wedding of his brother Kevin.

Burham will depart Missoula after the wedding and "hot foot" south to beat winter. With an estimated 2,250 miles to go, he expects to reach Mexico in six months.

It's a challenge, with a lot to gain, he explains. "Peace of mind, satisfaction of knowing that I did it."

Hikers see beautiful country that car travelers miss. By taking the time to see things, he appreciates them more, he said.

The idea for the cross-country hike goes back to Burham's Navy days. A few friends planned to hike the Appalachian Trail on the East Coast but "it never panned out. I've kind always had it in my mind that I wanted to do this," he said.

Burham, a sociology major at the University of Montana, served four years in the Navy. For two years he was a member of the Seal Team on underwater demolition squad. He also spent time in Vietnam.

The route Burham selected took him across British Columbia to Jasper, Alta. He took the Skyline Trail south of Jasper and

It was awfully good to be getting this close to home. I only had a few miles left. I don't think my feet even touched the ground coming into Missoula. What a welcome! I left a scorned Vietnam vet and returned a hero. My friends had always supported me. Now acquaintances who disparaged my service admired my achievement. And total strangers who didn't know me at all were in awe. I had successfully formed a new identity for myself.

I was so happy to see my mother and brother after all this time. My mother told me I was thinner than I had been when I left. That didn't stop me from kidding her about it. I absolutely loved being able to have dinner and stay with Mom and Kevin again that night.

Some friends had a surprise party for me the next evening. Many wonderful people showed up, including Buzz Blastic and his wife Beth, and my former boss Doug Bitney and his wife Nancy.

I connected with Debbie, the journalist at the *Missoulian* who I had met as she was bicycling back from Flathead Lake. She interviewed me for an article in the paper. I could not get over what a fuss people were making. I had started this walk for my own private purposes, and now everyone seemed interested.

I had planned my hike to make it back to Missoula in time for my brother's wedding. I spent the next few days helping Kevin get ready. He asked me to be his best man. The wedding took place in Rose Park on the 14th of September. The weather, which had been chilly, rainy, and cloudy, cleared up for that particular afternoon. It was just beautiful for their wedding. My cousin Ivan Lorentzen came down from Kalispell to sing for them.

After the wedding, I spent the next couple days getting ready to leave again. One of my errands was to go to the Missoula Bank and thank them for doing such a fine job of managing my checking account to fund my trip. I had had my checkbook with me the entire time, and when my amount of cash got low, I would go into a local bank, cash a check and buy $300 worth of traveler's checks. If that local bank questioned the balance in my account, I had the phone number for the Missoula Bank and suggested they call there and ask for Jack. He had been so helpful validating all my checks since my hike started, so I was glad to be able to see him while I was in Missoula and thank him personally. I also got a lot of camping supplies and a new pair of boots. I spent time breaking them in, hiking to the "M" on Mount Sentinel and all around Missoula. I had them to the point where I didn't think they'd give me any blister problems. I also made a temporary tube of Bag Balm to lube up hot spots on my feet.

A friend showed up at Mom and Kevin's place that afternoon. I showed him one of the wedding pictures, and he asked who invited "Jeremiah Johnson" to Kevin and Jeannie's wedding. I did look pretty wooly.

Before I left, Doug Bitney offered me my job back at the spa, with a bit of a raise once I got home after my hike. I was glad to have that possibility as I thought through my options. I was still meditating and walking, still trying to figure out what was next for me. My mind always came back to "teach without teaching." I knew I didn't want to be a teacher, but I had not figured out alternatives.

Tuesday morning, September 17th, My mother made me a gigantic goodbye

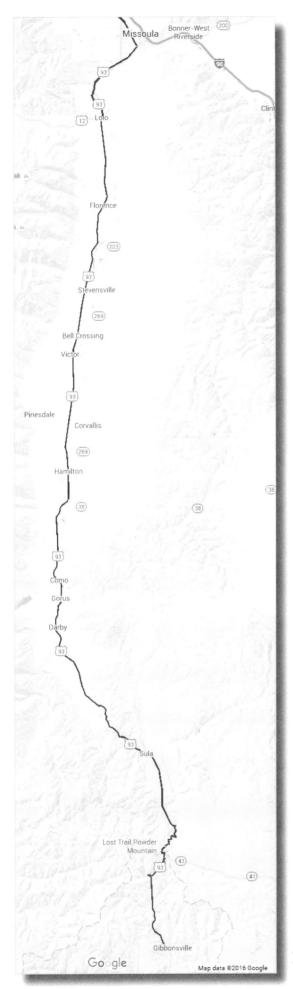

breakfast that was more than I could eat, as usual. Unfortunately, as I took off, I left her tearful in front of the garage. We had to say goodbye several times, not easily.

Getting out of town was just as hard, because every few hundred yards, I would get stopped by a well-wisher. I loved every minute of that. I got to see some people I hadn't seen for quite a while, including friends, co-workers, and fellow students. It seemed everyone saw me in the paper and just stopped by to say goodbye and wish me well. Buzz and some of his high school students got into his car, met me on the road, and cheered me on. It was fun to let them know that their teacher, Buzz, started this hike with me.

It was a very beautiful day, made all the nicer by spending it smiling, waving, and shaking hands. It's funny, but talking to these people, it was almost as though I was making the trip for each one of them. There always seemed to be something in what they said or in the looks they gave me that conveyed they'd like to try something like this, too. Perhaps there is a yearning in everyone to make a long journey, not just across miles, but in our souls. I was very grateful that I had the courage, motivation and the opportunity to do it.

The new boots worked great for about the first 20 miles. After that, I did get a little hot spot on my heel, but I didn't think it was going to be any big deal. I kind of figured that there would be something like that. Late that afternoon, Gyla, my former girlfriend who had been one of the first to welcome me home, brought me a nice dinner after I was a little over thirty miles south of Missoula. It was good to see her and her kids again. She also brought me my old boots, so I could wear them the next day. She was going to take my new ones to a sporting goods store and have the interior heels pressed out where my hot spots were.

I spent the night back on the road by the Bitterroot River just off the Stevensville cutoff. I had loved being home, but I was also very happy to be back on the road. I was only half done and was eager to finish my hike and finish what I set out to do. I was far enough out of town to be anonymous again. It was just the sound of my boots on the road, the occasional passing car, and my thoughts.

Heading due south of Missoula for the next few days, I enjoyed the picturesque Bitterroot Mountain Range and the Bitterroot River that flows through the valley.

On the morning of September 18th, the river was covered in fog in the morning, due to the temperature difference between the water and the air. It had gotten pretty cool the previous night and there was a thin sheet of moisture on the tent. It was a reminder that it was time for me to hurry south.

I packed the tent a bit damp, grabbed a granola breakfast and was on the road at about 8:00 a.m. It was another beautiful day. By the time I got to Victor, I was a little bit hungry, so I stopped at a local store for orange juice and yogurt to tide me over until I got to Hamilton. When I got there, I stopped at the DQ for something a little more substantial. The hot spots on my heels appreciated having my old boots on. They were a little tender, of course, but that didn't hinder me at all. I decided to press on four miles south of Hamilton to a little campground called the Angler's Roost.

My route took me through the Bitterroot Valley, carved by the Bitterroot River.

Traveling on foot took several days, but it was a short ride by car. Gyla brought me dinner again. She was really spoiling the hell out of me with fried chicken and goodies that really hit the spot. She also brought my new boots back after having them worked on. She told me she would try to catch up with me a couple days later at Lost Trail Pass and bring me dinner again, but she said that she wasn't certain she could make that one.

On the morning of September 19th, I was up about 7:30 a.m., ate what was left of the dinner, and headed out. The new boots felt good. On my way to Darby, I met a guy by the name of Henry Furnace. He was a nice, elderly gentleman, who said he was a rancher and a horseman from the Como Creek area. We had a nice talk about the weather, horse packing, backpacking, and the history of the Darby region of the Bitterroot. I enjoyed my conversation with Mr. Furnace very much and was glad to be back to one of the great joys of walking; meeting people by chance and enjoying a little conversation. That could never happen in a car or even by bike.

When I got into the little town of Darby early that afternoon, I went to a place called the People's Market. I met a couple guys, Terry and his younger brother Phil, who were friends of Gyla's. Terry ran People's Market, and Phil was the butcher. I wound up staying with them for the remainder of the day. Terry took me out to his place, and I was able to get cleaned up and get some rest for that afternoon. I caught up on my journal and studied some of my maps of the area. They were awfully nice folks. When I first got there, Phil was cutting some meat in the back, and we had a nice talk about

Trapper Peak near Darby, Montana.

113

Sunrise over the Bitterroot river.

the fact that he likes to ride ten-speed bicycles to stay in shape and take trips. He then asked me about my trip. I spent that evening right above the market in an apartment that Phil owned, getting to bed early for a great night's sleep.

The next morning, September 20th, Phil and I got up fairly early and went across the street for breakfast. We talked for a little while, and he wished me well. Then we went back to the market, and I got to say goodbye to Terry and was on the road at about 8:30 a.m.

It was a beautiful, sunny morning, and the trees were starting to change colors. A stream followed the road, and birds were singing. A little after 9:00 a.m., a pickup drove up and pulled off to the side of the road. The driver, Rich Anderson, had read about me in the *Missoulian* and wanted to meet me. He had walked to the Darby area all the way from Chicago and soon would be on his way to Seattle after earning a little money working for a local farmer. He had lived in the city all his life and was eager to do some farm work and see what that was all about during his walk. We shared experiences about walking and I was happy to meet someone who knew what a long trip on foot was like. I gave him Buzz's address in Missoula. To this day, I don't know if he looked him up or not. I enjoyed meeting Rich, and I'm glad he took the time to find me.

The sun was shining and there was just enough of a breeze to keep cool. The scenery was beautiful along the Bitterroot. This part of Highway 93 follows the Lewis and Clark Trail, which is marked with signs along the highway with different historical stories how their trip was progressing. It was kind of fun to be traveling about as fast as they had.

114

Fortunately, every time I'd get a little thirsty or hungry, a store would pop up. I enjoyed talking to people at the stores and on the road. Later in the afternoon, I stopped at the local ranger station and talked to the head ranger there who told me about a place called Indian Trees Campground just a few miles up the road on the way to Lost Trail Pass. I spent the night there and I had the whole place to myself. It was a rather cool evening, heading up toward the mountain pass.

The morning of September 21st was rather nippy, which was to be expected at that elevation. I was glad for my good repaired tent and down sleeping bag, and had a great night's sleep. From where I was that morning, the road got a little bit steeper until I crossed over Lost Trail Pass. It was a 7-mile stretch from the campground where I stayed to the summit. When I got to the top, it was so warm that I stopped and changed into my shorts. Then I started down the other side of the mountain. My next stop was a little

town called Gibbonsville, Idaho, where I got my next meal. I enjoyed meeting an elderly gentleman who told me a few stories about Idaho during the mining days.

Not too long after that, Gyla caught up to me once again. It was good to see her. I wanted to get a few more miles in that day, so we went down to a place called the Lewis and Clark Monument. It wasn't much of a monument, just a rock, but there was an access road that went up onto a little platform off to the side of the road where I could set up my tent. Gyla brought me a delicious dinner. I was grateful she had come this far from Missoula, but I hated to think about her driving all the way back to Missoula alone in the dark.

I thought about seeing Gyla again when I finished my hike, but as things turned out, I never go the chance to do so. Events intervened and my life took a different direction.

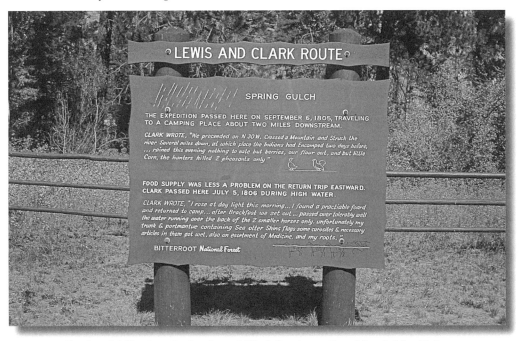

I enjoyed following the Lewis and Clark Route south as I headed for Idaho.

CHAPTER 6
Lost Trail Pass to the Utah Border

Sunday, September 22nd, I took off fairly early, stopping at the little town of North Fork, not too far from where I had camped the previous night. I was able to take a shower and get cleaned up at a truck stop. After that, I ate the rest of the food that Gyla had brought the night before.

I was descending from the mountains to walk along the north fork of the Salmon River. The countryside was starting to dry out where the river flows through a town called Salmon, Idaho. I didn't know where I was going to be staying, but a very nice elderly couple from California in a little pickup and camper said they were staying at campground in town. I went there and found a little patch of grass that the owners let me pitch my tent on. I had an awfully good dinner and then got caught up writing in my journal before I went to sleep.

The morning of September 23rd, Monday, I spent running around town and getting a variety of things done. I

The Salmon River in Idaho.

A view from the Lost Trail Pass in Idaho.

washed my clothes and had some steel taps put on the heels of my boots to see if they would cut down on the wear a little bit. I had a good breakfast and lunch in Salmon before I hit the road. It was about 12:30 p.m. before I took off, so I did not plan on making too many miles.

When I arrived in the town of Tendoy, Idaho, the only store had closed about a half hour before I arrived. A man by the name of Larry Bagley had a ranch just adjacent to Tendoy, and he invited me to his ranch for a spaghetti dinner. I respectfully declined because I didn't want to impose on Larry or his wife during dinner time. He told me about a rest area just down the road a mile and a half or so. I walked there and was in the process of pitching my tent when Larry

drove up in a pickup truck. He'd gone home and come back with a half-gallon of orange juice, some ice cream, brownies, and apples. It was unbelievable; he had a whole big bag of goodies that his wife had fixed for me. Wow! I was almost embarrassed that they were so hospitable. I got his address and promised to write him and tell him how my trip went. Larry was very interested in it.

The evening was getting a bit chilly, and I saved some of the goodies Larry brought and had them in the morning. The next morning, September 24th, I took off and reached the little town of Lemhi, in pretty short order. It wasn't too far down the road, and I had changed into my shorts while I was there and bought some milk and other goodies to top off my breakfast. Next, I headed for the town of Leadore. I planned on getting there by about 4:30 that afternoon and resting up for the next stretch I had to hike, which was quite a long one between Leadore and the Mud Lake area. I filled my canteen in Lemhi and took off.

About a mile outside of Lemhi, I stopped to take a leak, undid my hip belt. Since I just had my wallet tucked into my shirt and the only thing that was holding my shirt together was my hip belt, my wallet fell out. Sadly, it wasn't until I got about four miles down the road that I discovered that I had no wallet. Of course, all my money and you name it was in that wallet. I stashed my pack off the side of the road and started walking back to where I took my leak. This was much more frustrating than that lost bracelet trip. I was certain, though, that I remembered where I dropped the wallet and hoped that I could recognize the area again. When I got there, I hadn't remembered that the weeds were so thick or that water was running through there, too. I tried separating the weeds and hoping that if my wallet got in the water, it hadn't floated away. I spent about 15 minutes thrashing through the weeds about ten yards on either side of where I thought I had dropped it. I had almost given up when I then had an extremely lucky break and finally found it. Thank God! What a relief that was. I was ecstatic about finding my wallet and was also disgusted with myself for dropping it in the first place.

I started back to my pack thinking about the miles that I had lost, but then I decided to put the bad thoughts behind me. Words can destroy and words can build; even words you say to yourself. So I changed my thoughts from being angry about my wallet to enjoying the beauty of the day. I took my shirt off, caught some rays walking back, enjoying every minute. I got to my backpack, threw it on, and headed off for Leadore again.

I hadn't walked too far with my pack when I came across a farmer working by the road. I chatted with him for a little while about farming and how dry it had been this year. He was nice enough to then give me some water as he told me about how that highway used to be a train track back in the 1920s and early 1930s that was changed into a highway in 1938. He had lived there his entire life and entertained me with a history lesson about the area.

One of the great pleasures of walking is the chance to see beauty — not just the grandeur of the mountains, but the tremendous beauty of the details of the landscape like these Indian Paintbrush flowers along the side of the road.

About half an hour later, I started down the road again. A white van pulled up and the driver offered me a ride. I explained to him that I was just walking, and we talked for a little while. He introduced himself as Randy, a "tramp miner" who moved from mine to mine looking for work. He said he was checking out something in Bannock where he heard they were thinking of reopening one of their mines. He gave me some coffee, and we talked for a little while. He then wished me luck before we said goodbye.

A short while later, Randy drove up on me again. He had gone ahead to Leadore, bought some milk, pop, and some other things, and came back to give

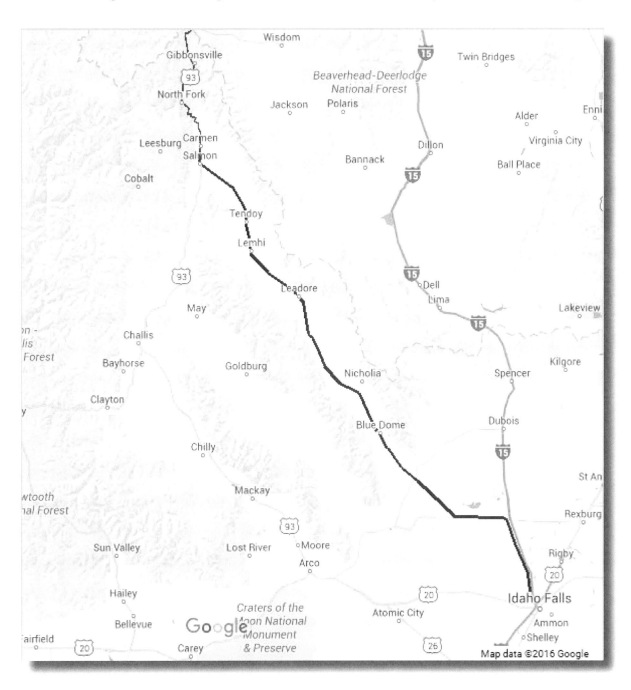

them to me. He was a really nice guy and I really appreciated his help on a hot, thirsty day.

I finally made it to Leadore and got more to drink and got a good dinner. I had to backtrack to a campground that was right by the rodeo grounds. Because they had a sheltered kitchen, I didn't even bother pitching my tent that night. I was pretty tired when I finally lay on my sleeping pad on the picnic table and slept. I was cold, even with my down sleeping bag, because of cold air circulating over and under me on that picnic table

On the morning of September 25th, I filled up with water and got a great breakfast in Leadore. The people at the store gave me some valuable information about the next stretch of road and a weather report saying it was going to be hot.

I left town at about 9:30 a.m. and it was already was warming up. I was glad for the little streams I ran into outside of town. I had packed about a gallon and a half of water, but it was not enough. About 15 miles into the day, a guy by the name of Hirsh Kolp from Boise, Idaho, stopped to talk to me. He thought my trip was great. He was very apologetic because he didn't have anything for me to drink and I was pretty thirsty. I had a little water left at that point, but I knew it wasn't going to last for too long. He said good-bye, wished me luck, and took off.

I didn't know if I would ever get to see him again, but a few miles down the road he left cans of beer and encouraging notes on several mile posts. Even with the rest of my water and the beers, the remainder of the day left me thirsty. I couldn't drink all the beers he left me—I needed water.

The Salmon River flows through some dry country.

I came across a windmill that was pumping water into a cattle tank. I was extremely thirsty, so I ended up taking a big drink from the cattle tank. As a result of drinking from the streams and the cattle tank, I got a minor case of dysentery. I couldn't help myself from drinking because it was so hot and I was so thirsty.

I continued to walk that evening well after dark and wound up getting about thirty-six miles or so from Leadore when I crashed for the evening. I pitched my tent by the side of the road and was shivering a little bit because I hadn't stopped to put my coat on. I got into my sleeping bag and tried to get warm, which is hard to do when dehydrated. I was exhausted, however, and fell asleep, despite the discomfort.

On the morning of September 26th, I woke up even more dehydrated and knew I had to do something. I made it to the town of Lone Pine at about 10:30 a.m. and took one of five rooms at the Lone Pine Motel. I showered and just drank all kinds of water. I spent the day there recuperating, drinking, sleeping and staying warm. I didn't feel better until dinner time.

I woke up pretty hungry. Unfortunately, the nearest café was two miles down the road, so I had a good walk over to the Blue Dome. I had just finished eating when a guy came walked in dressed in biking shorts and shoes. He ordered dinner, and I introduced myself. He was Tom Amberson from Pocatello, Idaho. We enjoyed sharing stories of our trips and he invited me to stay with him when I made it to Pocatello.

The 26th was a restful day in Lone Pine. I started feeling much better, having gotten through the dysentery

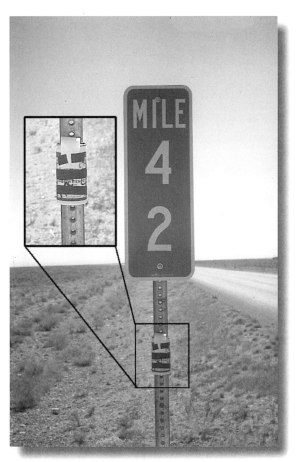

One of Hirsh Kolp's beers left for me with a note of encouragement taped on a mile marker in the desert.

and dehydration. On the 27th, I set out again, but not in too much of a hurry. It is a funny thing in small town America; everyone seems to know everyone else. I stopped in a local store owned by Verge and Edna Houcks. Their daughter ran the Blue Dome where I had eaten dinner. They knew Hirsch Kolp who had left the cans of Budweiser on the mile markers for me. He had bought the six pack at their store. I bought some snack stuff and said goodbye to the Houcks. I then walked the two miles back to the Blue Dome and ate breakfast there. I also filled up with water again and left at about 11:30 a.m.

The next town, Mud Lake, was about thirty-three miles away. The sun was shining that day and a good wind

The prairie becomes drier and drier until it is nearly desert.

was blowing. Fortunately, it was at my back and blew me right down the road. A few miles later, I started running into Hirsh's beers again. As glad as I was to see them, even though I knew I couldn't afford to drink all of them. So I took a few sips of the ones I didn't drink, and I really enjoyed the little notes. One was "keep on trucking," and another was "just a little something to get you down the road." Wow!

As I came over a hill on the road to Mud Lake, I was confronted by an amazing thirty-mile straight stretch of highway heading down the hill. It went down a little bit and dipped some and stayed just as straight as an arrow. I would pass mile post after mile post, and it didn't seem like I was getting anywhere. Luckily, with the wind at my back, I was making pretty good time, and it was cool enough that I didn't need nearly half of

the water that I had packed, which was nice. As soon as I realized that I was going to make it to Mud Lake without needing all of it, I began to get rid of the water to lighten my load. It was dark by the time I was about ten miles from town, but I just kept walking. I didn't like walking after dark on a busy highway because it was kind of treacherous. Cars couldn't see me. I needed to make the distance, so I stayed far on the shoulder and continued walking until I got to Mud Lake.

By the time I got to the town, almost everything was closed. I knocked on a motel office door, and a lady came to the door. I asked if there was anywhere I could pitch my tent for the evening, and she just directed me to a little stretch of ground on the other side of her hedge. That worked, so I crashed there. Since I was very tired, I slept extremely well in spite of the fact that there was frost on my ground cloth and tent the next morning.

On the morning of September 28th, I got up and walked about a block down the street to a little café called the Oasis and had a good breakfast. The locals were all drinking coffee and talking about their crops and cattle. An elderly gentleman came in and wanted to get into the bar adjacent to the café. He was told that the bar was still closed, poor fella.

I filled up on water a couple miles from Mud Lake in a town called Terreton and continued on to the junction of the Interstate.

The Mud Lake and Terreton areas were really an amazing example of what can be done with irrigation. The local people took their water from Mud Lake and used it to water enormous wheat fields; truly huge big operations. It was one of the most fertile areas I thought I had passed through on the whole trip. By the looks of all of the equipment in the yards, the farmers were doing quite well.

Just after leaving Terreton, I found my last beer from Hirsh on a mile marker. He wished me well and said goodbye and that was kind. His notes of encouragement were something I will never forget. I thought about the power of words. Those insults against Vietnam vets and the harangues of anti-war professors had done so much to drive me down. On this walk, a note and a beer taped to a mile marker or a shouted cheer from a passing car had the opposite effect. The idea of "teach without teaching" came to mind again as I meditated on my walk. I didn't want to be a teacher, but I did want to use the power of words to somehow help people who were struggling emotionally. I had pulled myself up on this walk, but not by myself. Countless strangers and many, many acts of kindness had pulled me up, too. I felt I had discovered a real

This road went so straight for so long that I seemed like I was standing still,even though I was streadily walking. As we say on the SEAL Teams: "A long as it takes; as long as it goes."

power that I wanted to put to good use in my life.

I got to the Interstate and found out that in Idaho, pedestrians are not allowed on the roadway. I had no choice but to walk on the frontage road for a while until that ended, and then I just walked in the ditch alongside the road until I got to the town of Roberts.

In Roberts, I had a good late afternoon dinner, for which I was very thankful because I was quite hungry. After that, I wound up walking down a little road that paralleled the railroad tracks. I walked that until the sun was about to set and just pitched my tent right there by the tracks. While it would have been much easier to walk on the Interstate into Idaho Falls, I was stuck taking the access roads to avoid trouble with the local authorities.

My night went pretty smoothly until about 2:00 a.m. that morning when a freight train came rumbling by. My tent was only about 20 feet from the track itself. Boy! I thought the Day of Judgment was here. It was a very rude awakening. I thought my journey and my life were all over.

A memory flashed before my eyes of an operation in the Mekong Delta. Our SEAL platoon was on a mission to capture members of the province level Viet Cong infrastructure. Because it was the dry season, we were moving through a dry rice paddy with no cover. Suddenly, a Viet Cong popped up out of a spider

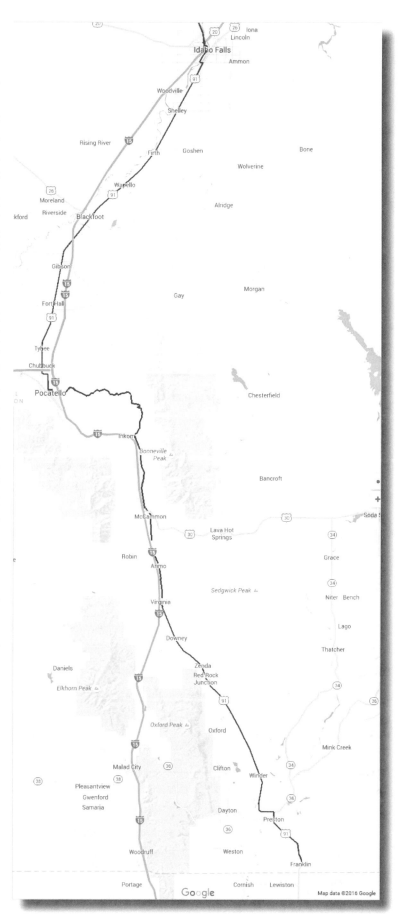

hole in the tree line about 40 meters away. He had his hands up, but because of the thick undergrowth, I couldn't see his hands clearly. Suddenly, he began firing at me, and I dropped to the dry earth and began firing my M60 back at him. He stopped firing and I assumed I had killed him, but just as I started to breathe again, the whole tree line lit up like a string of Christmas lights and we were taking heavy fire.

Another VC popped up out of a spider hole with his hands up and started doing the same thing as the first one had. Green tracer rounds zeroed in on me, and I thought for sure I was going to die. One round went through the ammunition cylinder of my M60, in the process setting off a tracer round in it and starting my M60 on fire. A couple other rounds hit my M60 instead of me, saving my life. The M60 burned intensely enough to singe my eyebrows, and a couple of VC rounds that hit the M60 burned my arms. Although I kept squeezing the trigger reflexively, the M60 had become inoperable.

Another SEAL Joe Hulse, who was nearby, yelled at me, "Leave the gun! You need to get the hell out of there!"

We were heavily armed, but we were also seriously outnumbered, so we had to call for a chopper. I tried to get the M60 working again, not wanting to leave my weapon behind. Hulse hollered again for me to leave the damned gun and get out of there.

A couple other SEALs had managed to capture the second VC, and they handed him over to me. The only weapon I had now was my survival knife, which I showed the VC to let him know I meant business. LT Ganoung, my commanding officer and best friend, ordered us to fall back across a canal where there was more cover and where the chopper would pick us up.

I hauled the prisoner across the canal to the pickup zone, and the platoon laid down suppression fire as the Navy Seawolf chopper came in. It was amazing that the helo crew decided to come in despite all the enemy ground fire.

We loaded up, and as we took off, Chief Bill Bruhmuller asked me where the prisoner was. I replied, "We're sitting on him, Bru."

As we lifted off, green tracers were floating around us like confetti. When we got back to base, though, we found the chopper had a few holes in it from enemy fire. We couldn't believe the chopper had stayed in the air. To this day, I thank that Seawolf crew for coming in and saving us. What bravery!

Just as suddenly, I was back by the railroad tracks in Idaho. Training is never over, I thought to myself. I realized that my Vietnam experiences and the stresses of them were still with me and were still something I would have to deal with. I now know flashbacks such as these are part of PTSD, but back then, I still worried a bit that they were just a little bit part of me being crazy. As the train rolled off into the distance, I tried to get my heart rate back down to normal and eventually got back to sleep.

I woke up the next morning, September 29th, I got all packed up and I walked the eleven miles to Idaho Falls on an empty stomach. By the time I got there, I was definitely ready for breakfast. There was a KOA campground on the northern end of town where I stopped for milk and other goodies to tide me over. I took a shower and washed my clothes. I then headed in to the center of Idaho

Falls, stopped at a restaurant and pigged out.

It was a nice, sunny day. With a clean body and clothes and a full stomach, I felt good. I really enjoyed walking through cities on Sundays because they were very quiet, without many people or much traffic, making for a nice, mellow trip.

I ended the day in Shelley, Idaho, just a few miles south of Idaho Falls. I put up my tent and spent the night in a city park across the street from the Walker Café, where I had a good dinner. At about 1:30 a.m., there was another rude awakening when all the park sprinklers came on. The tent kept me dry and the sprinklers didn't give me a Vietnam flashback. About an hour later, I can vaguely remember hearing the sprinklers shut off, and then I went back to sleep.

The next morning, September 30th, I had a good breakfast at the café and then went back to the park, packed everything up, and headed south again.

I reached the town of Blackfoot, Idaho, at about 2:30 p.m. and met some awfully nice people in a grocery store there. They were very inquisitive about my trip and gave me a self-addressed envelope and said that I should tell them how it all turned out after I finally made it to Mexico.

The steel taps that I had put on the heels of my boots in Salmon didn't work worth a damn, so I went to a shoe shop in Blackfoot and replaced them with nylon plates. Thankfully, these worked pretty well and eliminated about a week's wear on those heels. When putting on miles like I was, a week's wear is very noticeable. The shoe repair man was an elderly gentleman, and it took a while for

The prairie stretches out in all directions, offering not an inch of shade to a hiker.

me to get the message across, but he did a really good job on the boots.

I left Blackfoot at about 4:00 p.m. and headed for Fort Hall, Idaho, an Indian reservation. When I got there, I stopped at a post office in the corner of the laundromat owned by a guy named Ron who offered to let me pitch my tent just outside.

The next day was an easy day, as I was just going as far as Pocatello only ten miles away. I was also looking forward to seeing Tom Amberson, the bicyclist I had met in Lone Pine at the Blue Dome diner. I caught some breakfast at the Fort Hall Café and talked to Ron for a little while again before leaving.

When I got into Pocatello, I looked for and found the Mountain Folk Equipment store where Tom said he worked. He wasn't there when I arrived, but the guys there let me set my pack in the corner, while I walked over to the University of Idaho to see if I could find Tom. He had told me about the Outdoor Club on campus and I thought they might know where Tom was. I spent some time seeing the University, but still didn't find Tom. I washed some clothes and got something to eat before returning to Mountain Folk Equipment.

Tom showed up shortly thereafter, and we went down the street, had a couple beers, talked for a while, and then got a pizza. I really enjoyed the fact that Tom, like me, was a very outdoor-oriented person. I ended up spending that night with Tom on the floor of the Mountain Folk store, which was in an old building downtown.

I decided to rest and stay in Pocatello for another day to let some of my sore spots rest for a while. That morning Tom and I had breakfast at Elmer's Pancake House. All the other guys from Mountain Folk were there, too, so it became kind of a gathering of the clan. It also sounded like an executive board meeting because they were talking over things that they were planning to do for the upcoming ski season. They talked about their plans for a cross-country ski school that Tom was going to head up like he had the year before.

Later on that afternoon, Tom and I borrowed his sister's car and drove out to Arimo, a town about thirty miles south of Pocatello. Since I couldn't take the Interstate south of Pocatello and I wasn't sure of the route I should take, he showed me the way on the back roads.

That evening we caught the movie *Jeremiah Johnson*. I had seen it before, but it was a good flick, and we both enjoyed it very much. I thought of the people back home in Kalispell who said I looked like him.

On October 3rd, the next morning, we had breakfast together at a local café, and then I said goodbye to Tom before I took off. Leaving nice people behind is always a bit difficult.

It was a cool, overcast day. I started walking the route Tom showed me the day before. The day turned kind of chilly late that afternoon and it began to rain. With it raining hard, I stopped in the town of McCammon for dinner, hoping it might taper off while I ate. It didn't, so I just kept walking to Arimo.

I arrived about 7:30 that evening and warmed up in a café. Thank goodness, it was still open. I asked the gentleman who seemed to be running the café if there was anywhere around there that I could spend the night and get out of the weather. He referred me to the nearby gas station. I went over there and met the owner, Mr. Con Thomas. He was nice enough to let me know about a little sheltered shed that he had out behind his house where I was able to spend the night warm and dry.

The next morning, Con's wife gave me four apples, and I talked with her for a little while before I left. I then went back to the station and thanked Con for his hospitality. He was really supportive of my trip. He had also done quite a bit of walking and hiking around the hills around Arimo, so he really appreciated what I was doing.

It was a beautiful sunny morning, and I was feeling really well when I headed out on the road again. I had to stay on an access highway because I still couldn't get on the Interstate. The road ran parallel to the train track, and I waved at the engineer in a moving train. The engineer motioned for me to come hop aboard. I moved my arms like I was running to catch up to the train. We both laughed at each other, and I saluted him. We were both waving at each other as he rounded the corner and the rest of the train clamored by.

Later, I stopped in the town of Downey, had a little yogurt and some lunch and continued walking. At the little town of Swan Lake, I grabbed a V8 dinner. I didn't have much to eat that day, but the weather was nice, and I enjoyed my walk immensely.

Darkness had fallen when I got south of Banida. I saw a light on at a farmhouse and thought I would see if I could stop there. I walked up as people were just pulling out in a car with their entire family. I spoke with the gentleman who was driving and asked him if there was any place that I could spend the night. I think I probably looked kind of fearsome to him in the dark. Even though he didn't quite know what to make of me, he directed me to the Mormon church, just about a block away, where they said I could pitch my tent in a wheat field adjacent to the church yard.

They were having wedding when I got there, so I had a bit of an audience. I answered a few questions about my trip and wished them well.

On October 5th, I was up early after a chilly night and was back on the road by 8:30 a.m. The sun was shining, and the morning was cool. It was only about seven miles to Preston, so I had breakfast there in a coffee shop in the Burnham Hotel. Just down the road, I caught an ice cream cone on the way out of town. Not too far down Highway 91, I stopped in a little drug store in Franklin, Idaho, just before crossing the Utah border. I got some Kleenex and toilet paper in there and had an opportunity to meet and talk with some nice folks at that place.

CHAPTER 7
Across Utah to Arizona

I crossed the Utah border near the town of Richmond. I was really impressed with how beautiful that farming country was. The next town I came to was Smithfield, Utah where I intended to spend the night. I stopped at a Conoco station near the edge of town and asked the guys working there where I might be able to pitch my tent and camp in town. They directed me to a city park that wasn't too far away. I thanked them for that valuable information. They let me leave my pack there with them so I could go next door and have some dinner and do some writing in my journal.

Back at the station, I talked to the guys about my walk. I told them normally, I would get between three and six ride offers a day, but that day I had ten, which was really unusual. I joked that I had been wearing my long pants, so I wondered if it was my legs that were scaring people away on those other days.

I took my pack and pitched my tent in the Smithfield City Park, and then I walked down to one of the local pubs, had a beer, and watched TV for a little while.

On October 6th, Sunday morning, I was up early and on the road by about 7:45 a.m. I got breakfast seven miles further on in Logan, Utah. It was another chilly night and morning, so I had a nippy walk to Logan. That breakfast wasn't enough. I came upon a Sambo's café a few miles

later and stopped for a second strawberry waffle.

After that, I headed south again, stopping at the Western Park campground to shower and take the chance to wash my clothes. By then, the sun was high and it was a really pleasant, warm day. I passed through Wellsville, Utah where I stopped and had a sandwich. It was a small world, as one of the elderly gentleman at the restaurant was at the wedding a couple nights previous at the Mormon church where I camped in Banida. While we were talking, his wife came in and asked him why he wasn't at home watching the Mormon Church Conference. His response was that he was already adequately "spiritually fed" and didn't want to overdo it. What an interesting guy.

From Wellsville, I started over a little mountain pass, and the reds, oranges, and yellows of the trees were breathtaking. When I got to the summit, I changed into long pants because the sun had gone down and it was beginning to get a little cooler. I met a guy by the name of John Williams in a 4-wheel drive who was taking some pictures of the area. He was from Salt Lake City, gave me his phone number, and asked me to give him a call when I got there.

It was just about dark when I came to the town of Mantua, Utah. I met a guy who owned a campground where

Beautiful farmland in northern Utah.

he said I could pitch my tent. He wanted to make sure I felt at home. I had put in quite a number of miles that day, so I was anxious to get my tent up and get to sleep. Since it was another cold night and I didn't have a hood on my sleeping bag, I put my balaclava on and cinched my bag up around my neck. That way I stayed warm all night and had a very cozy night's sleep.

The next morning, October 7th, I found a good deal of frost on the tent. As I was packing everything up, I met a guy who was staying adjacent to me in a Winnebago, and he brought over some hot coffee, and we talked for a little while. I sought out the owner of the campground to thank him for giving me such a nice place to stay.

By the time I was packed up, the sun was up, and it was beginning to warm up. I walked four miles to Brigham City for breakfast at a small downtown café that had fantastic food. I was really impressed with Brigham City. It was incredibly neat and well-kept. It looked like I could have eaten off their sidewalks. The temple is quite an amazing structure, as well.

After breakfast, I headed out, going through Perry and Willard on my way to Ogden. I arrived there about 6:00 p.m., had some dinner and changed into long pants, since when the sun set, it cooled off pretty quickly.

Ogden was the biggest city I had hiked in so far. It was getting dark by the time I got to the other side of town. I saw a motel that said it had hookups for campers, so I asked the guy there about pitching my tent. He said that would cost me $5 or I could have a room for $8. I figured what the hell and sprung for the room.

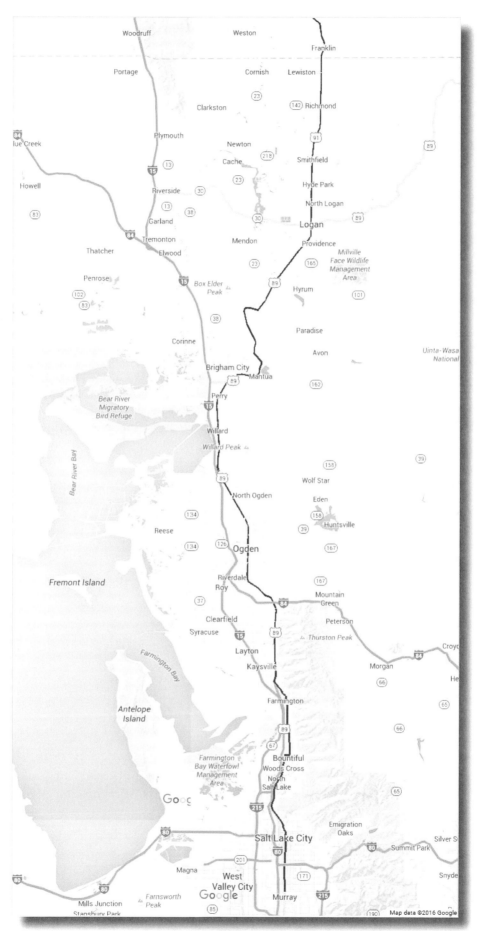

I checked in, left my pack and headed for an Albertson's just across the street. I got some ice cream and cookies and came back to the room to watch a Monday night football game. What luxury.

The next morning, October 8th, I had still more Ogden to hike through. I hopped on Highway 89 going south and was impressed by the amount of traffic. I stopped at a gas station along the way, chatted with the elderly gentleman who ran it, had a little snack and headed out. A few more miles down Highway 89 I turned onto Highway 106 and away from the traffic. I next went through the little towns of Farmington and Centerville on my way to Bountiful.

It was great when I finally made it to that town. When I got there, I called Lon, a guy whom I had met earlier in the trip and who gave me his Salt Lake phone number, to just say hello. I had no idea where I was going to be spending the night. Since I was right next to a local police department building, I figured they would know where I could legally camp. I went in and asked one of the sergeants at the desk. I told him about my hike, and after we talked for a while, he asked me if I wanted to stay with them that night in the jail. I said, "You bet." It was clouding up and looked like it was going to rain all night, so I thought this was going to be a nice dry evening at no cost. I told the officers I hadn't eaten dinner yet, and they said I could leave my pack there, and they would find me a cell when I returned. I joked they were very civilized because they locked people up by appointment.

I had a good dinner at a nearby café and dessert at Baskin-Robbins before returning to the police department. I talked to the policewoman on duty for a while, and then she took me back and locked me up for that rainy evening. I left my pack right outside my locked cell door, and got a great night's sleep.

The next morning, I woke up and made some noise on the cell door to get some attention. An officer came back angry and asked me, "Why the hell are you making all that noise?" I told him I was ready to leave and get some breakfast. He looked at me like I was nuts. Apparently, no one had told him about my stay and he thought I was a criminal. He told me to shut up. I pointed to my backpack and asked him to please call his night shift coworkers because they had invited me to stay. He just took off and left me there.

I lay back down to wait and see what was going to happen next. On one level, it was a bit comical, but I was anxious to get going and worried I would stay locked up longer than I wanted.

It took almost an hour to finally get everything straightened out. The officer came back and reluctantly unlocked my cell door. As I was leaving, I thanked everyone on duty for my dry evening. Some of them were even smiling.

I took off and headed south for Salt Lake City. I spent the day walking, and made it to the middle of the city at Temple Square. As I was taking pictures, an elderly gentleman walked up to me, and we talked for a little while. He was from Salt Lake and had visited Kalispell, Montana and as going to retire there.

I walked south through the heart of the city during lunch hour and got some weird looks for my wild appearance. I was kind of freaked, too, because I hadn't seen that many people in a long time.

I stopped in a sporting goods store called Timberline Equipment to get some

132

The Mormon Temple in Salt Lake City.

to get a picture of me and my pack and write an article for the *Tribune* about my hike. After he interviewed me and got my picture, we found out that we were both Vietnam combat veterans.

I called Lon again, and he came to the store, picked me up, and took me to Gerhard's house in southern Salt Lake City. Gerhard was the German man I had met up in Canada just before crossing the border. I took him up on his offer of the use of his house while I was in town. He wasn't there, but was working up at the Snowbird Ski Area.

I then went to a café a few blocks from Gerhard's house, had dinner, and went back to take a shower and wash my clothes.

The next morning October 10th, I took my boots down to a nearby shoe repair shop to have them resoled. The tire rubber had really held up well. I wanted new tire treads, thinking that they would probably last me all the way to Mexico from here.

After breakfast, I ran some more errands and eventually stopped for lunch. I then spent that afternoon at Cottonwood Mall getting some other things I needed. Later, I took a local bus over to the *Salt Lake Tribune* building to finish my interview with Craig. When we finished, he took me to his house to have dinner and meet his wife, Becky.

Later that night, after I got my boots, Lon picked me up, and we went to the Tabernacle to watch the Mormon

freeze-dried meals, fuel for my stove, and other supplies. A guy came into the store and asked loudly, "Who does that big backpack by the door belong to?"

I came over to him and told him it was mine. He then asked me, "What the heck are you using it for?" I let him know that I had walked here from Alaska with it. He, had an amazed look on his face, and after a brief period of silence, he told me that he was Craig Hansel, a sports journalist for the *Salt Lake Tribune*. He was very interested in my trip, and the more we talked, the more determined he was

Choir practice. He then took me back to Gerhard's for another good night's sleep.

On the morning of October 11th, Craig came over, picked me up, and we went up to the Snowbird Ski Area. What an impressive place! Gerhard was working as the engineer, helping them design and build their tram lift. It was great to see him again and catch up on both our lives since we had met at Glacier Park. He told me that he had taken me up on my offer of hospitality in Missoula and spent some time with my family as he drove south. We rode that to the top of the mountain where I met Liam Fitzgerald, the chief ski patroller.

Craig took me back to Gerhard's house. I had a chance to give my brother Kevin a call. It was great to hear his voice, and he let me know how he, Jeannie, and Mom were doing.

On the morning of October 12, Lon picked me up again and took me back to the Timberline Equipment store, and I started my hike again at about 9:00 a.m. I headed south out of the city and got to the town of Draper. From Draper, I took a mountain dirt road that went through the Traverse Mountains to Alpine. From there, I went through the town of American Fork. On the outskirts, I struck up a conversation with

a gentleman who was watering his front lawn. I asked him where the nearest police station was so I could find out where I could legally camp. He sent me down the road. As I was walking, a guy by the name of Howard Adams drove up and said that I could camp in his back yard. It wasn't too cold that night, and they were very nice folks.

At this point in my hike, I was very eager to simply get on with it. I had accomplished so much. I had grown physically and emotionally strong. I

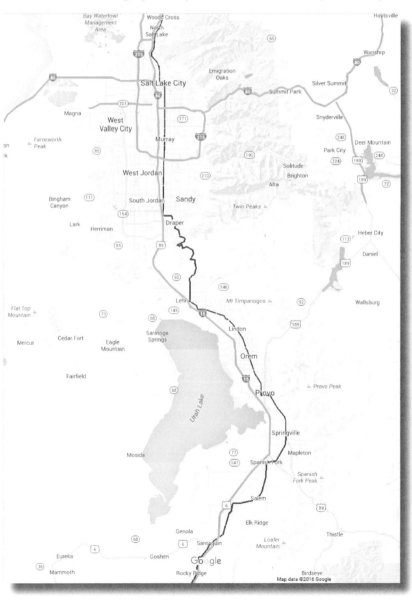

134

This Guy Has 'Sole'

He'll Walk a Mile?
No, Many Miles

By Craig Hansell
Tribune Sports Writer

Greg Burham likes to walk.

He likes it so much, in fact, that he is walking from Alaska to Mexico.

"I was in a SEAL team in the Navy and I had planned to hike the Appalachian Trail but everyone faded," Greg said. "I have always wanted to do something like that so I sold my car and started walking by myself.

"I started at Hyder, Alaska, a small gold town in the Panhandle, and walked through Jasper National Park in Alberta, Canada. I prefer to stay on mountain trails or back roads away from highways," he continued.

High Point

"The high point of the trip has to be the people, all types from all walks of life. It has really been nice."

Greg is making between 25 and 30 miles a day carrying a pack weighing 55 to 80 pounds.

"I spent the night as a house guest of the Bountiful Police Department in the jail. It is an interesting place at night. My admittance card was misplaced and it took about half an hour for them to check me out."

He is having his third pair of boots resoled while he is here.

Only Ride

"The only ride I have taken in the entire 1,900 miles of the trip was in Canada. My boots fell apart and my feet got infected so I took a ride into a small town to heal and buy boots. When I got the new boots I took another ride back to where I stopped walking and began again.

"I was going to walk through Nevada but I thought the scenery would be better in Utah and I was right, the mountains here are great.

"I was amazed at the number of people I saw on the trail. I met some guys in Canada that were horse packing to the Yukon. All summer long, fully 90 percent of the bikers I met were Americans."

Much in Common

"I have a lot in common with the horse packers and bike riders. They can appreciate my speed of travel.

"I was two days south of Missoula, Mont., when I met Rick Anderson who was walking from Chicago to Seattle. He was raised in the city and had always wanted to see the country and experience farm life. He was walking across the country, taking his time, working on farms and experiencing a new lifestyle. He had always wanted to drive a tractor and a combine. When I talked to him, he had done both."

"You have a lot of time to reflect on a lot of things while you are walking. There is time to talk to people. Everyone is interested in talking about themselves and I have become a student of people.

"I talked with an elderly fellow in Salt Lake near the temple and found out a lot about the buildings in the city.

"I met a guy named Hirsh Koip in Idaho while I was walking across a desolate area. He said he was sorry he didn't have anything for me to drink and apologized for it. I told him I had plenty of water and I was fine. After he left he drove into the next little town and left a message at the store for me to watch the mileage posts along the road. He had bought a six pack of beer and taped a can and a note on every mile post along the road.

Great Gesture

"His notes said things like 'keep on truckin'. The gesture was great.

"Everyone seems to assume, if they take a trip like this, they won't be well received but people have been incredibly nice.

"I think it has a lot to do with the way people travel. By car, everyone is in their own little womb, the Winnebago generation. The most important part of a trip like this is just going.

"Don't be over prepared.

"When Anderson left Chicago he had $90 in his pocket and some clothes. If you wait until the time is right, you probably won't go.

Boots Important

"Boots are the number one priority. I've been getting 600 to 700 miles to a pair of soles."

Greg, 25, calls Missoula, Mont., home and expects to be finished in two months.

"I should have close to 3,000 miles under my soles when I finish. I plan to continue south along old highway 91.

"Salt Lake is the biggest city I have been in and it is hard to get used to the fumes and the cars.

Greg Burham
Walks Alaska to Mexico

Oct 15, 1974
Salt Lake Tribune

knew I would make Mexico without a struggle and that psychologically, I was in a much better place. I had a deadline to get to Missoula for my brother's wedding and I was eager to get to Salt Lake to see my friend Gerhard. But that was all behind me. Now, between Salt Lake City and Mexico, there was just road—many miles of it for me to cross. I had just a few more milestones ahead: Seeing my friend Dick Martin in Jerome, Arizona and then seeing my SEAL swim buddy George Ganoung in Tucson. I started putting in long days to make the miles.

The next morning, October 13th, I met Howard's wife, Peg, and she fixed me a really good breakfast before I left and was on my way by 9:15 a.m.

I spent most of that day passing through the cities of Orem and Provo, and

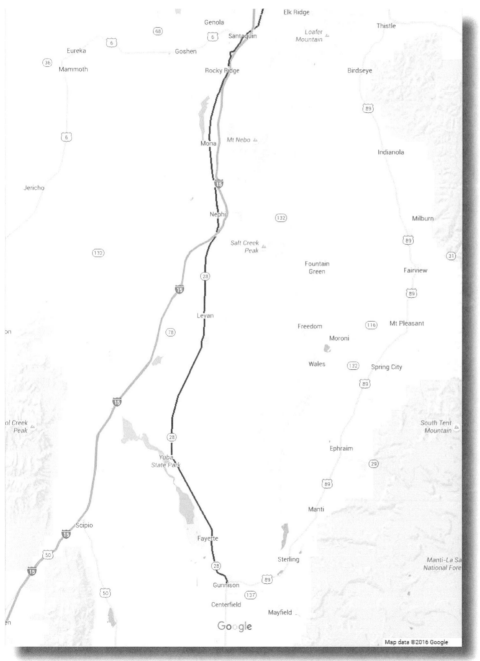

since it was a Sunday, it was a very soothing, mellow walk. While there, I made a pit stop at an ice cream parlor and inhaled my usual pint.

I stopped that evening in Spanish Fork, and after dinner, I found an extremely nice campground called the O'Brien Trailer Park. The lady who ran it was extremely pleasant and friendly. I was able to wash my clothes and take a shower.

On October 14th, Monday morning, I got a rather late start from Spanish Fork. I hung around for a while talking with the lady at the campground who told me how to make fruit leather and gave me three rolls of peach. It was really good stuff, and it paid off because my hike south of Spanish Fork was

136

one of those long desert stretches, so they really came in handy. She also told me that most Mormons have approximately a three-year reserve supply of food, which is kind of amazing. The Mormon folks that I met and who helped me seemed to be together about a lot of things. What the specifics are of their belief system, I'm not sure, but the practical applications seem to be pretty impressive.

When the day was over, I wound up having hiked about 36 miles, the last seven in the dark. I was awfully tired by the time I got to the town of Nephi. Dinner was the first thing I did after I arrived. I then found a reasonable motel room and crashed there. I needed a good night's sleep that night and got it. My legs, my left foot, and my lower back were a bit sore, so I was going to make some changes the next day with how I carried my pack and laced my left boot.

My nose was sunburned, too. But other than that, everything was spiffy.

The next morning, with a good breakfast, I was feeling pretty hale. I bought some leather oil for that boot, saturated the crease in the left foot and laced it differently, which I hoped would help. I then took off to Levan, a distance of about eleven miles, where I had a little lunch.

The next town, Fayette, was 26 miles down the road. Most of the distance between these towns was quite long and dry. It was about 9:30 p.m. by the time I got there. Since I didn't find anything in Fayette, I decided to push on to the next town, about five more miles further.

It was about 11:15 or 11:30 p.m. by the time I finally reached Gunnison, my latest night yet. I didn't relish walking in the dark because it was hazardous with the cars and everything. Even though I

The stark beauty of the desert mountains of southern Utah.

carried a little hand flashlight, I still didn't feel very comfortable.

Fortunately, there was a café still open in Gunnison, so I was lucky enough to get a piece of pie and a cup of caffeine-free coffee. When I went to the city park, there were "No Camping" signs all over the place, so I ended up crashing just across the street in a gas station trailer park. Since there was nobody up at that time of the night, I figured I could settle everything in the morning.

I sweated and shivered most of the night because I pushed it a little bit too hard that 42-mile day in the desert. I didn't blame myself because I knew that it was just one of those days that there was nothing to stop for, so I just kept going.

The next morning, the guy at the gas station trailer court was really nice and didn't charge me anything. He wished me well on my trip.

Before leaving Gunnison, I stopped in a local bank and had some more money forwarded from the Missoula bank because I was getting a little low in that department.

In light of the long day yesterday, I decided to just make it an easy day and only walk the fourteen miles to Salina. When I got there, I found a little trailer park where I could pitch my tent, get a shower and wash my clothes. I found a shoe repair shop and had another nylon tap put on the heels of the new soles that I got in Salt Lake City. I had my fingers crossed, hoping that they would help the soles last a little longer. I caught up on my journal and took it easy for the remainder of the 16th. After having a day full of good meals, I even considered catching a movie that evening, but sadly they only had showings on the weekends. I ended

The post office in Axtell, Utah just south of Gunnison.

up watching part of a high-school football game, and then I turned in.

On October 17th, I had a good breakfast at a place call Shaheen's Café. I was talking to the man who ran the place, and he told me about a guy who had walked around the world had stopped there in Salina and stayed for the night. He was so impressed with my hike that he ended up buying me breakfast.

I left Salina to make the 18 miles to Richfield, feeling wonderful after having such a good night's rest and great meals. The fact that it was a beautiful sunny day helped, too.

Utah's hunting season was beginning that weekend. I was passed by quite a few California trucks and campers that looked like they were heading up to hunt.

When I reached Richfield, I was able to get a nice lunch and then rested until about 3:00 in the afternoon, with the weather still really pleasant. I walked on into the little town of Elsinore about eight miles down the road.

That day a few people pulled over, offered me a ride, and I chatted with them. One of those guys said that he was a traveling salesman who had passed me two or three times in the course of his travels, and curiosity finally got the best of him, so he finally pulled over. We talked for a little while.

On the way into town, a gentleman who was about to take a bike ride suggested several places around town where I could spend the evening. It turned out that he was the mayor of Elsinore, and he said if anybody gave me any trouble, I

Big Rock Candy Mountain did not look a bit like candy.

was just to send them straight to him. He was really a nice guy.

A little farther down the street in Elsinore, some local ladies were having a hunter's bake sale. They were in the process of setting up, so nothing was yet available to buy. One of the ladies must have seen how I was eyeing her wonderful big sugar cookies. Noticing my disappointment, she gave me one. I offered to pay her for it, but she insisted that it was free. She was nice, and so was the cookie.

I then walked across the street to a small grocery store and grabbed some milk and yogurt. As I returned to the bake sale, they were raffling off a rifle, and they asked me if I wanted a ticket for that. I thanked them, but I respectfully declined and mentioned that since I was walking, I had no desire to carry a rifle.

As I was sitting there enjoying my milk and cookies, one of the bake sale ladies came over to talk. She was a bit stern and was very much concerned about me taking care of myself and keeping my parents posted. I assured her that I was enjoying myself very much, and that everything was fine. We parted smiling.

I made it to the town of Sevier after a 30-plus-mile day. As usual, in a day that far, the last few miles I walked there in the dark. Fortunately, I just caught one of the local restaurants still open. The lady in there was nice enough to make me a cheeseburger before she closed up. Her husband owned the place, and after he and I met, he let me camp just outside on a stretch of grass. The next morning, October 18th, I had breakfast in their café. They had just opened it having moved there from California.

The owners of the B Motel and Cafe treated me to an enormous lunch.

I headed south from Sevier and very soon came to Big Rock Candy Mountain. I had seen pictures of that and heard stories about it since I was a small child. Several tourists were there. I didn't really see where they got off calling it Big Rock Candy Mountain--it was a dry hump of rock like so many others. Anyway, I had an expensive milkshake before moving on to Marysvale. I came upon B's Motel and Café, and met the owner sitting outside with his daughter. They treated me to an enormous lunch of a big cheeseburger, a salad, a piece of apple pie, and some milk.

A couple miles outside of Marysvale, I was stopped by a van, and the gentleman at the wheel offered me a

John Bammes, a local school teacher, gave me a history lesson on this area of Utah.

ride. I thanked him and explained that I was just walking, and he thought that was a pretty neat idea, so he pulled over, and we talked for quite a while. His name was John Bammes. He had been a school teacher in the area and proceeded to give me a history lesson of that area of Utah.

I reached Junction, Utah after dark and ended up camping beside a Texaco gas station run by a young guy who was very hospitable and friendly. We talked for a while about my walk and how his business was picking up as a result of the hunting season opening.

When I left town that morning, I knew it was going to be a long day. Fortunately, about six miles later, I got to Circleville and had a good brunch to fuel me for the 30-mile stretch to my destination Panguitch. I filled up myself and my pack with water before I headed out. A river flowed alongside the road, but I remembered the dysentery in southern Idaho. The river went through quite a few pastures, so though I stopped to dunk and cool myself in the stream, but I didn't drink any of it.

About ten miles outside of Panguitch, I met a hitchhiker at a junction in the road. As we talked, the sun set. He was a ski patrolman going to apply for a job at Snowbird. I told him to look up Gerhard.

Not long after that, I made it to United Campground a couple miles north of Panguitch. Some nice people there offered to give me a good deal on a place to pitch a tent, which I accepted because I was tired. I decided Panguitch could wait until tomorrow.

It was the time of year when the days were warm, but the nights were frigid. That morning, I had to breathe on the tent's zipper to get the frost off and

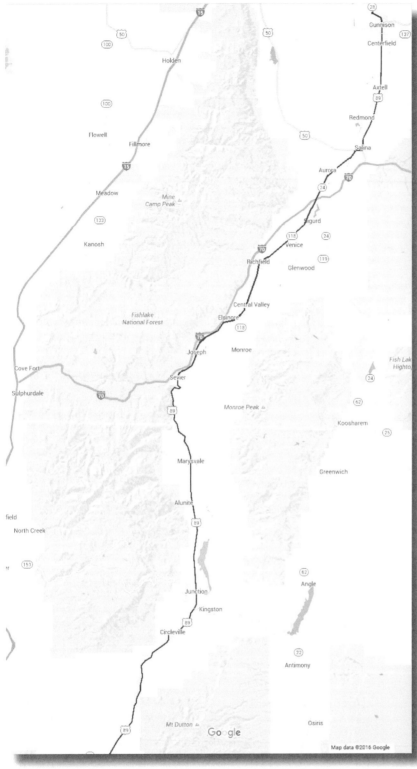

out and got some ice cream and cookies and watched a Sunday afternoon football game.

On October 21st, Monday morning, I had a good breakfast in Panguitch and took off about 9:30 a.m., having enjoyed my motel stay very much. The sun was out, but it was windy, which made it a bit chilly. Unfortunately the wind was blowing right in my face, making even the downhill grades somewhat difficult.

I had lunch in Hatch, and then headed for Long Valley Junction, hoping to spend the night there. When I arrived, I discovered that nothing was open. There wasn't even a place to get some water. I ended up going into the woods and pitching my tent. My dinner then consisted of two fingers of peanut butter and just enough water to wash it down, saving some food for breakfast.

The next morning, I finished all the food I had and got on the road at about 8:10 a.m. It was about fourteen miles to the next town, Glendale. About two miles out, it began to rain, just a sprinkle. No big storm ever materialized, for which I was very grateful. The road did look as if it had rained pretty hard the night before.

About ten miles down the road, I ran across a KOA. I thought that was

get it open. I walked the remaining few miles to Panguitch and I checked into a motel room. I needed some good meals and a good rest. I slept most of the day. I called home that afternoon and had a wonderful talk with Mom. Then I went going to be a real oasis until I found that there was no one there to open it up. There was a little sign on the door saying that business had been slow and to check at the adjacent trailer house. I did that, but there was no one around there, either. I did find some water and drank as much as I could to fill the void and filled my water bottle, too. I was hoping I could find a meal soon.

When I got to Glendale, the only thing there was a grocery store. I just bought some peanut butter, crackers, yogurt, milk, and Hostess Cup Cakes to tide me over.

Just outside Glendale, a gentleman drove up in a Datsun pickup and introduced himself. He was a nice guy by the name of Bill Jettle. He asked me, as a number of folks south of Salt Lake City had, if I was the guy who had walked here from Alaska. Evidently, he had seen that *Tribune* article. We talked for a little while, and he wished me well on the trip and drove off. A few miles later, in Orderville, I saw Bill again. I walked right by his house when he happened to be in his garage, so he invited me inside for coffee and pie and introduced me to his wife. We all had a nice chat. He told me of a good campground at a place called Mount Carmel not too far down the road. Evidently, he called ahead and told them I was coming, because when I reached there, they knew who I was and were very friendly. Amazingly, they only charged me a buck to stay there that night. I showered and walked the mile down to the junction for dinner and to do some writing in my journal, too.

While I was in the café, it started to drizzle, so I ran back to the campground only to find that I had pitched my tent right under a big neon sign. Since it was

Long Valley, Utah near the border with Arizona.

143

still raining, I couldn't well take it down and re-pitch it. Instead, I moved it to the other side of the restroom building and tied it together enough so the rain wouldn't get in. I hunkered down in my sleeping bag for a good night's sleep.

The morning of October 23rd turned into an extremely pleasant, scenic day, which I enjoyed very much. During breakfast at the Mount Carmel Junction, it was a little overcast, but the weather improved as the day went on. I went over a beautiful mountain pass through gorgeous red rock formations. I was sorry that I didn't have any film for my camera.

The road I was on went right between Bryce and Zion National Parks, but I didn't take the time to see either one of them.

On the outskirts of the town of Kanab, I saw a place that advertised that they made Grand Canyon float trips. I stopped and asked for some information about if I would be able to make it through the canyon at this time of the year. They said they were pretty sure the trail was still open. They wished me luck on the trip, and I headed on into Kanab. I had lunch there as it started to rain. Luckily the rain quit just as I finished eating.

CHAPTER 8

Making It to Mexico

With the rain clearing, I set off again and crossed the border to Fredonia, Arizona on a beautiful sunny afternoon. Moments later, however, it began to rain again. The weather is quite changeable in the desert.

I pulled up to a Highway Department booth check-in station. I talked to a gentleman in uniform by the name of Mr. Ford. At first, he seemed a bit skeptical of my hair and general appearance, but after we talked, he got by that and let me use his phone to call the local Forest Service office to find out if the Grand Canyon Trail was open. It was. Mr. Ford referred me to the sheriff's office in Fredonia and said they could probably find me a place to stay.

The rain let up as I walked to the sheriff's office. In what appeared to be a combination police, fire and town hall, I met the sheriff himself, an awfully nice guy by the name of Cecil Cram. In the back of his office was kind of a recreation room for the fire department. He let me roll out my sleeping pad on the concrete floor of the rec room. I could sleep there that night in a nice, dry place. Since it continued to rain that night, it was great to stay dry.

I went across the street, got some milk, cookies, and ice cream and pigged out that night. I was able to get a lot of my gear squared away and dried out in the rec room. I also patched my tent that night

with glue and rip-stop tape, even hand-sewing part of it, and got it back together again. It had never been the same after falling down the cliff and sailing across the lake. I was hoping to keep it enough together for the trek across this last state.

On the morning of October 24th, I got up fairly early and because there is an hour difference between Utah and Arizona, it was even earlier than I thought. I ate breakfast across the street and mailed a post card to Dick Martin in Jerome, Arizona. Dick was the hitch-hiker I had met near the Columbia Ice Fields in Canada who had walked to Banff with me. I wanted him to know where I was and approximately when I would be getting to town.

It was a tiring 30 mile climb from the desert floor in Fredonia to the top of the Kaibab Plateau (at around 7,900 or 8,000 feet elevation), making for a long day. The scenery was spectacular. The higher I climbed, the more it looked like I was traveling in the mountains of western Montana, with the tall ponderosa pine among the aspens. The top of the Kaibab Plateau offered truly stunning views.

I finally got to Jacob Lake as it was getting dark. I was a bit surprised that it wasn't a town, just a hotel and restaurant. I had a good dinner and hoped to get a room for the chilly evening, but they were a bit more costly than I anticipated. After dinner, I walked across the street and just

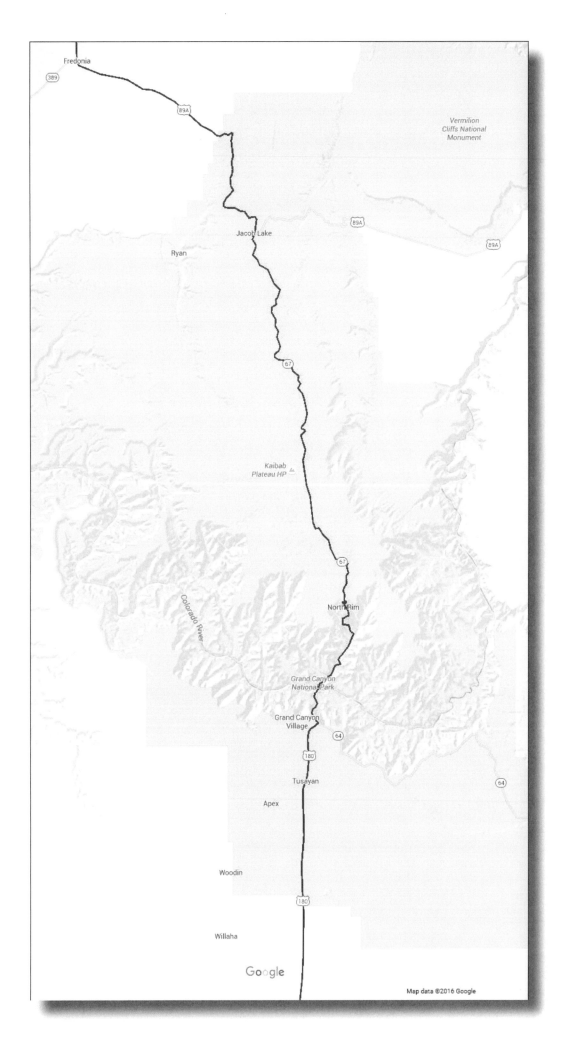

pitched my tent in the woods in a little campground. Due to the elevation, it was as chilly as I had anticipated and rained slightly, too. Still, I did get a good night's sleep.

October 25th was a wonderfully sunny morning. My tent was a little damp as I packed it up. I was hoping that the sun would last for the rest of the day to warm my walk. I had a great breakfast where I had had my dinner and left Jacob Lake.

I was eager to get as near as I could to the North Rim of the Grand Canyon that day. The breeze blew through the pines, the sun was shining and it continued to be a beautiful day. That weather and scenery made for a very pleasant walk. About 26 miles later, I found myself at the Kaibab Lodge area. Sadly, everything there was closed and boarded up. A nearby Conoco station was also closed, but, fortunately,

it had a water fountain that they hadn't drained yet, which solved a worry that I had. I went to a campground adjacent to the Kaibab Lodge, which was still open. I had one of my freeze-dried dinners that evening.

My target for the next day was the North Rim of the Grand Canyon. After a Grape-Nuts breakfast with water and powdered milk, I hit the road. The weather changed every five minutes, from sun, to rain, to sleet, back to sun, and then rain again. It was kind of confusing.

Thank goodness I reached the North Rim, or, as it was called, the head of the North Kaibab Trail, at about 2:00 that afternoon. The sign there said it was about fourteen miles down to the Phantom Ranch on the Colorado River. I fooled around that afternoon taking pictures because the scenery was just so unbelievably spectacular. Some miles

Walking through the Arizona desert with the Grand Canyon finally visible in the distance.

down the trail, I was finally able to see the South Rim of the Grand Canyon.

When I was about five miles from the ranch, it looked like someone was pulling a dark blanket over the landscape. The rain and lightning of the thunderstorm soon settled into the canyon. Seeing the lightning and hearing the thunder echoing in the canyon reminded me again of being in Vietnam when we received mortar and rocket fire. My heart jumped right up into my throat and that feeling of panic set in.

I picked up my pace to almost a run then, not knowing quite what to expect from the storm. I was glad that for a while, there was just enough light to keep from stumbling on the trail. It was getting darker and darker as I ran. I knew from SEAL training that panic is never helpful. The antidote is to put yourself a hundred percent into the moment, paying attention to dealing with the reality at hand, not some nebulous fear. I concentrated on where I was putting my feet, and kept an eye out for somewhere where I could get a little shelter. Soon after it got dark, I looked up, and saw a wall of rain was heading my way. I was still running when the rain hit me like a hammer.

Fortunately, about 20 yards later, I came to a rock ledge that provided me with some shelter from the rain, even though I was already wet. More importantly, I wasn't out in the open for the lightning. I was only under the ledge for about ten minutes when I looked up and saw the wall of thunder clouds pass over to the north. In just a few minutes, that the entire storm left the canyon; rolling off it as quickly as it had come.

As the clouds left that night, the three quarter moon right above the

Spectacular view of the North Rim of the Grand Canyon.

The Grand Canyon Lodge on the South Rim.

canyon gave me plenty of light. SEALs are used to moving at night. Darkness is our natural habitat and we feel safe and competent in it. The moonlit landscape was really beautiful. It was like a special gift just for me. Few people hike the Grand Canyon at night, and I must say, they are really missing something. Every time I would come around a corner, the moon would be gorgeously lighting up the canyon. It was breathtaking.

When I arrived at the Phantom Ranch by the Colorado River at the bottom of the Canyon, I found out that the only way to get dinner was to have a reservation. All I really wanted was a couple of sandwiches and a place to pitch my tent. I wound up paying a buck-fifty for a dry turkey sandwich. They definitely had the bottom of the canyon monopolized, so I had to take what I could get.

As I munched on that poor feast, a young gentleman and his two young sons from Colorado came up to talk to me. They had hiked down from the South Rim and were going back up the next morning. They suggested I stay in the barracks, since I couldn't find a decent place to pitch my tent. It was $4 for a bunk.

On October 27th, I left the ranch at about 7:00 a.m. in a light rain. I was unable to get even so much as an orange from the people who had sold me the awful sandwich the night before. I didn't have much to eat, but I figured I could make it anyway.

I had a misunderstanding in directions and got going on the South Kaibab Trail, which was wrong. I ended up taking about a mile loop and doubling back to finally get on the Bright Angel Trail. Despite the setback, it was a

The trail hugs the cliffs along the North Rim of the GrandCanyon.

View from the South Rim.

beautiful trip up. The higher I got, the more visible one of the most beautiful places on earth, the Grand Canyon, became, with its extraordinary mountains and river valley.

About three miles short of the top, my lack of breakfast caught up with me. I felt like the walls of my stomach were rubbing together, so I stopped and chowed down on all the food that I had left. It was just some honey, peanut butter, and a few raisins. It was enough and I got to the top at exactly noon according to my watch. I wasted no time going directly to the ice cream parlor that the guy and his sons from Colorado had told me about the previous night. They must have beaten

me to the top because I looked for them at the South Rim, and they were already gone.

I got a room for that evening at the Bright Angel Lodge and spent the afternoon washing my clothes. I packed in some good meals along with another visit to the ice cream parlor. I even had a couple beers in the lounge before I went to bed.

The morning of October 28th was cloudy and drizzly, with the weather report calling for up to six inches of snow. I left the Grand Canyon Village as it began to sprinkle, and quite soon after that, it began to rain heavily. It was so cold and the wind was blowing so hard that it made it a bad day for walking.

I made it about seven miles to a little place called the Moqui Lodge, and I was drenched by the time I got there. I waited to see if the weather was going to blow over. When it became obvious it wasn't, I got a room for the night and was able to dry everything out again. The room was a bit costly, but it was well worth it. I found a book there called *Survive the Savage Sea* and began reading that excellent, inspiring book. That night saw the first snow of the season. I was really glad that it was cold enough to snow and quit raining.

On the morning of October 29th, I had a good breakfast at the lodge and set out in the middle of the snowstorm that was pretty heavy at times. I walked through a few off-and-on breaks in the storm, interspersed with some hail, snow, and sleet for a little while, and then the sun would come out, and it would be beautiful. That morning, the snowflakes were very big, which didn't get me as wet as the sleet did. That sleet I could have done without because it soaked me pretty thoroughly.

I arrived in the little town of Valle that afternoon and found that all the tourist facilities were seasonal and they were closed now. A gentleman in a local campground allowed me to stay in an empty, unheated shed he had out front. Fortunately, that gave me enough shelter to get me out of the storm. I just slept on the plywood floor. I had a cold, restless night, so I didn't sleep very well. It continued snowing through till morning.

The morning of October 30th, my breakfast was a can of peaches that I got

A light snow up in Kaibab Pass.

151

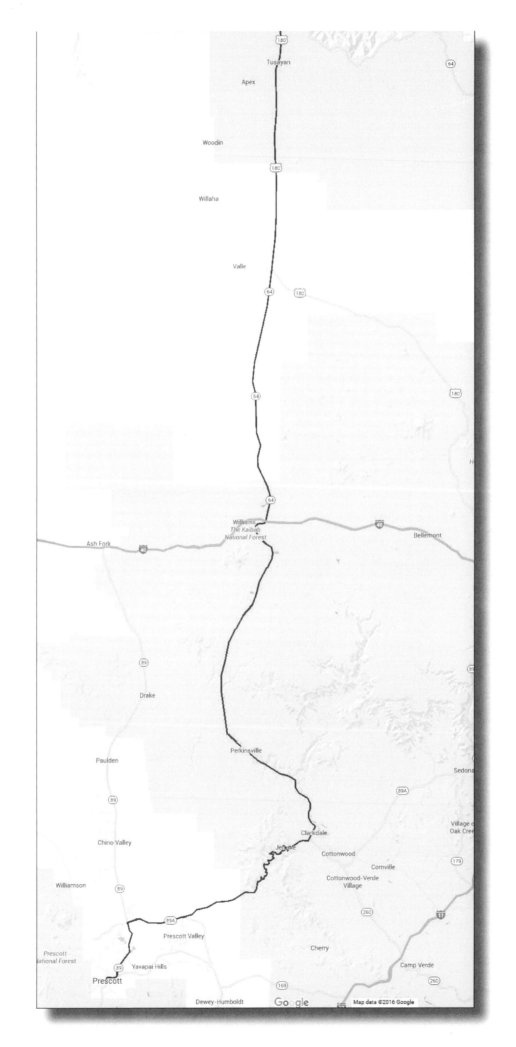

from the campground store. Fortunately, it stopped snowing at about 10:00 in the morning, but it was still quite chilly. The sun did come out for a while, and it was really pretty.

The manager of the ice cream parlor at the South Rim, a guy by the name of Scott, drove by me that day, and we talked for a little while, and he wished me well. He had remembered me eating all that ice cream.

Later that day, I arrived in Williams as the sun was setting. I then met a couple at the bus depot, Kevin and Theresa, who were hitchhiking all over the U.S. and Canada. Since we had all been to a few of the same places, we went to have dinner together to compare notes. It was the first real meal I had eaten since the morning before.

I checked into a motel and decided to stay there for a couple nights as the weather report predicted that the storm was due to get even worse the next day. My feet were rather sore at this point, too. I was glad that I was able to eat very well for the next two days. The motel room was small, clean, warm, and out of the weather with a great bed. I got everything clean and dry, and then I kicked back and watched TV and got a restful sleep.

I spent Halloween in Williams. I had a wonderful breakfast and then ran a few errands and asked some people about the best road to take to Jerome. Lunch and dinner were amazing, as well. Every day I hiked, I used a great deal of energy, and that made me feel good about myself physically and emotionally. Being able to eat in restaurants helped me fill my energy tank more completely than what I cooked for myself in the wilderness. I needed the calories and appreciated well-prepared meals.

That night, it didn't look as though that storm was going to quit, but it was time for me to move on. I caught an early breakfast and was on the road at about 8:15 a.m. the next morning. The sky looked stormy and threatening over the mountains where I was headed, but, fortunately, I stayed just below the storm in elevation. Quite a bit of snow remained on the road, but it didn't snow while I was walking. I had some peanuts and dried apricots in my pocket, and the only reason I stopped all day was to adjust my boots. I ate while walking and tried to make as many miles as I could that day.

Quite a few hunters were in the area, and I stopped to talk to a couple of them. One gave me a half-pound of bacon that I ended up leaving with Dick in Jerome. The road I was on was a relatively untraveled back road. I got in about 33 miles that day. At sunset, I made camp just below the Sycamore Canyon cutoff. It got extremely dark and threatening quickly that evening, so I pitched my tent just off the road, seeking shelter without delay.

I slept pretty well until about 3:00 a.m., when the rain cut loose in a downpour. I kept waiting for it to let up, but it never did. Rain on a tent is loud as all heck, so I didn't get much sleep. By the time I got up that morning, I was sleeping in a mud puddle, rather a sea of mud, which made for one of the more frustrating mornings I had had. Unfortunately, the heel taps the last guy who replaced my soles put on had worn down to the point that their nails were now working their way into my heels.

I took off in a mood as foul as the weather. It poured as I walked down to the Verde River and then began to climb up on the other side. The rain turned

Dick Martin set down his pack and I took the picture of him the top of the Mingas Mountain Pass.

to snow and sleet as I got up Mingas Mountain. It was foggy, and I was cold and drenched.

It was a difficult day and all that I had to eat was the remainder of the peanuts that I had in my pocket. I did make the 20 miles to reach Jerome. Fortunately, Dick Martin's wood shop was one of the first places I came to when I got there, and he had his stove cranked. I warmed and dried myself and my pack as Dick introduced me to his coworker, Leon, and one of their friends, Marty. For starting so nasty, the day really ended up very nice.

When I got warm enough, Dick took me down to Clarkdale to wash some of my clothes. I spent the night in an abandoned house after dinner at a local café. With the nice—and cheap—set up. I

decided to take the opportunity to stay in Jerome and have my boots resoled.

November 3rd, a Sunday, was a very restful day. It was still cold and rainy, so we cranked up the fire in the shop again. The people were extremely open, and it was quite a unique little town. Jerome was home to a community of young, very talented craft people with their own shops. They all seemed to be enjoying life and doing their own things. Every day we had wonderful meals at the Candy Kitchen.

November 4, after breakfast at the Candy Kitchen, Marty and I took Dick's truck down to Prescott to have my boots resoled. The tire soles I had on my old boots worked great, so I wanted to replace them with the same. I had Marty take me down to a tire place where they did re-treads and got a tire. Then we went to the shoe repair shop. The cobbler there was a bit confused when I gave him my boots and a tire, but he said he'd give it a try. As it turned out, he did a very good job on them.

I decided to leave on Thursday, and Dick said he wanted to walk with me from Jerome to the Mexican border. First, he had wood-framed mirrors to finish building so he could sell them to finance the trip.

On Tuesday, the weather began to break, and that afternoon became just beautiful. The sun was shining and I really enjoyed the view. Jerome is an old mining town stuck up on the side of Mingas Mountain, which overlooks Cottonwood and Clarkdale. I enjoyed being able to get a good rest, have great meals, and spend time with Dick and other nice folks. On November 6th, I called Prescott, but my boots weren't ready yet. I spent the day relaxing as I had the few days before. I got a tour of the Tally House, one of the historical sites in town that Dick and Leon had renovated for the Bicentennial. They had done an awfully impressive job on it.

Later that afternoon, I called George Ganoung in Tucson to say hello. He and I had gone through UDT Basic Training and UDT-22, and we went together to Vietnam with SEAL Team TWO. When I told him about my hike, he expressed an interest in meeting me somewhere along the line and walking the last few miles of the trip with me to Mexico. I had promised him I would give him a call when I got close and we would see how things went.

Thankfully my boots were ready on November 7th. Dick's friend Marty and I thumbed to Prescott to get them, getting a ride with a guy in a pick-up with a camper and a dog.

My boots looked great and I was very thankful for the wonderful cobbler who had fixed them. We then got a ride back to Jerome, had dinner again at the Candy Kitchen, and then spent the night on the Tally House lawn. When it began to rain, we went inside and spent the rest of the night on the floor of the house — very deluxe.

On the morning of November 8th, I hitchhiked down to Clarkdale to wash some clothes and then thumbed back up to Jerome. We had breakfast at the Candy Kitchen, and Dick took me around Jerome to see more craft shops and meet some new people. We then bought a few groceries and went to see Pat, a lady Dick was in love with, and had dinner there. She made chicken vegetable soup that was delicious. Dick and I planned to leave the next morning, so we spent that evening packing up and getting ready.

Breakfast was my last meal at the Candy Kitchen. I could see in my mind's eye my end goal. Mexico was days away now and I was really looking forward to finishing my trip.

Dick and I left town a little after 9:00 a.m., and through the use of a couple of steep shortcuts that Dick knew, we were able to reach the summit over Mingas Mountain about eight miles away in a couple hours. My boots were now a bit heavier, but they felt great.

It was awfully nice to have company again, but I didn't think Dick's heart was in the trip.

It was a beautiful day. The sun was shining, and from where we stood, we could see the San Francisco Peaks and the Flagstaff area.

That afternoon, we stopped for sandwiches along the road on the downside of Mingas Summit. My new boots seemed to be working very well, and the tire treads were giving me a bit more cushion. The hike was going to be a lot easier on my feet ankles and knees.

By sundown, Dick had indeed talked himself out of continuing the trip. He had only started with me because he had promised. Now, he really wanted to be back in Jerome. He had had a few productive days with the mirrors and was enjoying that work. Pat, his girlfriend was also there. He was very apologetic about not continuing with me, but I assured him it was no biggie. I was used to operating on my own by this point. I still hadn't resolved what was next for me, and I looked forward to having some quiet meditation time. I enjoyed Dick's company, but understood that Jerome was where he belonged. He didn't need

to hit the road to discover his place in the world.

We parted company at Prescott Valley, a housing development where he began thumbing his way back to Jerome. I don't think he had too much trouble getting a ride back as I continued on.

It was just me, the sound of my boots and the road again. I then arrived at the junction of Highway 89 well after dark and had a burger at the Pinion Pines Bar with a 7-Up. Highway 89 was going to take me through the town of Prescott and a number of other small towns on my way south to Wickenburg, Arizona. About a mile outside that town, I pitched my tent by the side of the road for the night.

After a bitter cold night, I woke on November 10th, having to breathe on my

The fishing wasn't very good the day I crossed the Hassayampa River south of Wickenburg.

156

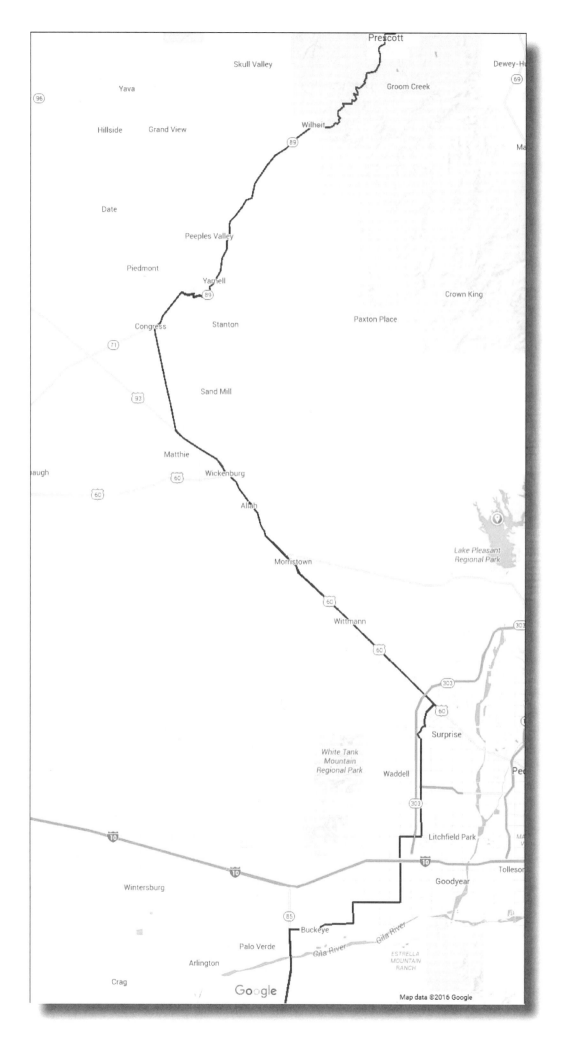

tent zipper to get it open. My tent and my ground cloth were crusted over with ice.

Within four-and-a-half miles, I wandered into Prescott in the sunshine. I walked through the town square on that beautiful day and saw the place where the fight scene from the movie *Billy Jack* (about a Green Beret Vietnam veteran) was filmed. I felt a certain affinity for that story about another Special Forces Vietnam vet.

After breakfast, I stopped at a nearby gas station and changed into my shorts. Outside Prescott, I headed uphill for a number of miles. I went through a pine forest until the downside of the summit where the trees began to thin out.

I then entered Nowhere, Arizona, and went into a little bar and had a sandwich with a 7Up. I told my story to the bartender, and he was amazed that I had walked that far only to get to Nowhere.

After sunset, I entered Kirkland Junction and had dinner there at another bar and restaurant. I put my tent up about 50 yards from the bar.

The next morning, November 11th, which was Veteran's Day, I climbed up from Kirkland Junction to Yarnell, where I had lunch. From Yarnell, I fell off the top of the plateau down to the town of Congress, about eight miles away, which was right on the desert floor. The elevation difference was amazing. I called it a day at Congress. At this point in my hike, I considered a 22-mile day an easy day.

I found a place just behind a gas station to pitch my tent. I was able to air out all my gear and catch a good dinner at the little restaurant nearby, and then enjoy a beautiful desert sunset that evening. I turned in early and had a very restful night's sleep.

I got up early, and I noticed the difference in nighttime temperatures between the plateau and the desert floor. No need to defrost my tent zipper. It had been a balmy evening, and the morning was just as pleasant—a nice change.

Nothing was open in Congress that morning, so I headed for Wickenburg, about sixteen miles away. Fortunately, I got an early enough start that it wasn't too hot by the time I got there. As usual, people offered me rides. I particularly remember elderly lady in a Jeep. She had a little sun hat on and sunglasses and kind of a light complexion with rosy red cheeks. I declined the ride and thanked her very much for stopping, and she just smiled sweetly and cranked that thing in gear and jumped off.

In Wickenburg, I caught a good brunch and then took off for Morristown only about six to ten miles away.

When I arrived, I found a little store and chatted with the lady who owned the place. She was kind enough to tell me about a KOA about three more miles down the road. When I left the store, it was already starting to get dark and the traffic on the highway made the walk nerve-wracking.

I arrived at the KOA about 7:00 p.m., got a spot, took a shower and washed clothes before going to bed. I slept on a picnic table under a shelter rather than hassle with my tent. I pigged out on food from the little grocery store at the campground.

The next morning I was headed down Highway 60 pretty early. After breakfast in Wittmann five miles down the road, I stopped and talked to some construction workers on their lunch break.

George snapped this picture of me outside of Ajo, Arizona.

We had a good chat about their work and my trip, and we joked about hippies, hard hats, and us Vietnam veterans.

Back on Highway 60 I hiked to Litchfield Road, took a right, and headed due south through very impressive farm fields all the way to Luke Air Force Base. Outside the gate, I stopped at a little shop and had dinner. South of there, at about dark, I arrived at an intersection with a lit sign that said Litchfield Park. I was able to flag down a sheriff's deputy and ask him if there was anywhere in the area that I could pitch my tent for the night. He told me "not in this area, because Litchfield Park is a closed community." He then said that I probably wouldn't find a place until I got down at least to Goodyear or a little beyond. I thanked him for the information and walked through Litchfield Park, stopping only

for a little food to keep me going. The road had an island in the middle of it and was lined with palm trees. The ice-frosted mornings were behind me.

I continued on to Goodyear. When I got there, I stopped at a police station for camping information. I knocked on the door, but no one answered. I waited for a little while, but since there wasn't a response, I just decided to take off.

I kept walking to Avondale, a town a couple miles down the road, and I stopped at Byrd's Mobile Park. The owner gave me permission to stay there. I didn't bother with the tent because the nights were so balmy, so I asked if I could just stretch out on his backyard. He was really hospitable and gladly gave me permission to do that. We had a nice talk about my hike before I had dinner at a nearby A&W.

Sunset at the Organ Pipe Cactus National Park.

The next day, I was lucky to have a pretty easy day hiking-wise. I just went from Avondale to Buckeye. I did have a little trouble finding a place to stay after getting turned away from a couple trailer courts. They were all set up to serve motorhomes, pickup campers, and things like that. They weren't willing to make a place just for a tent. I went to the city-county clerk's office to get some advice. The lady behind the desk got the sheriff on the horn and told him about my situation, and he agreed to let me stay in the jail. I made sure that everyone knew I was a guest, not an inmate. I spent the remainder of the day running errands, before dinner and a nice chat with the sheriff before getting locked up.

I got up awfully early the next morning, November 15th, and unlike my jail stay in Utah, I was able to leave before it was light. Thank you! After that, I had a great breakfast on the southern edge of town just as the sun was rising. I knew that I had about 33 miles to make that day to get to Gila Bend. It was going to be a hot long day, so I wanted to get some miles in while it was still a little cooler. I got 15 miles behind me by noon.

About 19 miles outside of Buckeye, I had some ice cream, drank some OJ, and talked with the nice people who owned the store. They were very curious about my hike.

When I got to Gila Bend, I phoned Mom. I was really glad to hear her voice because it had been a long time since I had talked to her. I also called George Ganoung, my SEAL buddy who lived in Tucson to tell him I was in Gila Bend. He said he and his wife would meet me the following day at the local post office at noon.

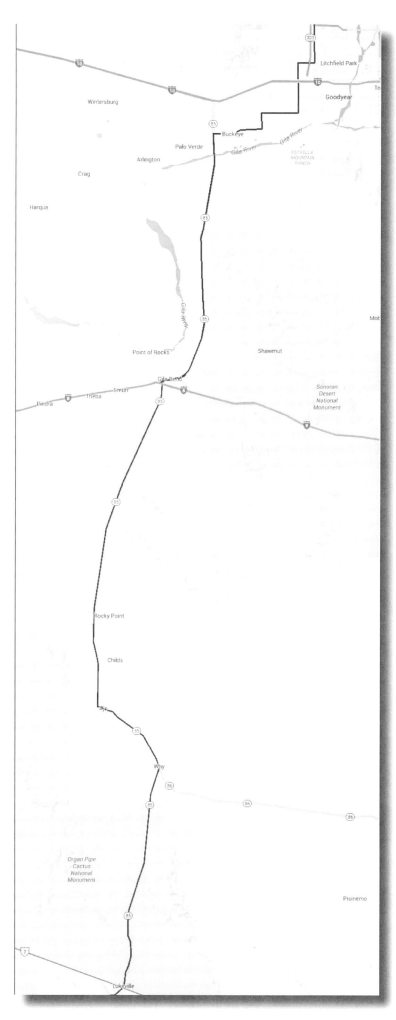

After spending the night at the Palms Trailer Court, I headed to the post office in Gila Bend to meet George and Maryleta. George Ganoung is a very special friend of mine. We went through SEAL training together and were both assigned to the same Underwater Demolition Team. When he transferred to the SEALs, I wasn't far behind him. In Vietnam we went through quite a few harrowing times together. I was really looking forward to seeing him.

When we met, it was hugs all around. Then we went back to the trailer court where I was staying so I could pack up my stuff. George announced he was going to make the last 80 miles of the trip with me. I was so honored to have one of my very best buddies with me for ultimate achievement of my goal. He was packed and ready to go already, having discussed the trip with Maryleta beforehand.

We said our goodbyes to Maryleta at the trailer court. She headed back to Tucson, and we were off to Mexico. We got off to a difficult start. We were so busy catching up with one another that we missed Highway 85. We tried a shortcut to 85, but that didn't work, so we had to backtrack to the intersection where we started.

We got lunch and finally got on the right road at about 12:15 p.m. It was really a great day to be able to share this experience with such an amazing buddy. I

Me outside the custom's office in Sonoyta, Mexico on George Ganoung's birthday: November 19th.

was impressed that George and I got 21 miles in that day. I was used to travelling on foot. For George, it was his first day and a long one, but he didn't complain. When we stopped, it was dark and cool. George told me he was pretty stiff and that he was seriously considering just thumbing back home from there. I knew he would not quit on me, no matter how sore he was.

The next morning, November 17th, we were up with the sun, and after a makeshift breakfast, we took off from our roadside camp. We packed a couple gallons of water with us, expecting a hot 21 miles to Ajo, our planned destination. Fortunately, there was enough cloud cover that we were able to make it to Ajo without too much water trouble.

About four miles before getting to Ajo, we stopped at a bar and had a

pitcher of cold spring water. It was really, really good. Coming into Ajo we found a Dairy Queen, so we stopped there and had a burger and relaxed for a while. On the other side of town we had a second dinner and watched the sunset. We put in another seven miles in the cool dark before we crashed by the road. George didn't talk about being sore or about quitting that second night; he was in it with me to the end.

When we woke up, we discovered a heavy dew had fallen during the night, making us wet and chilly. We waited for the sun to come up and warm us before we got up and packed everything still damp.

We hiked the four miles to Why, also called the "Y" because one fork goes to Mexico and the other to Tucson. We spread our stuff outside a restaurant to

Since this ws the end of my hike, the Mexican stop sign "Alto"made sense.

dry while we had a good breakfast. We made sure we had enough water when we took off. From Why, we were only 20-some miles from the border. The water bottle I had leaked and wasn't worth a hell of a lot, so I threw it away. We got a new gallon jug of water and took turns carrying it.

It was truly wonderful to be in the company of such a good friend. We talked non-stop. He asked a million questions about my walk, the physical challenges, the practical details, and of the Grand Canyon. He was planning to hike there himself.

One thing we never talked about was PTSD or its symptoms. PTSD was not a diagnosis in those days, of course. But we also didn't talk about nightmares, insomnia, anxiety, anger issues, suicidal thoughts or any other symptoms. You never wanted to show weakness on the SEAL Teams and those symptoms were wrongly considered flaws. I know now how important it is to talk things out, especially in a safe place like being with a good friend. We have worked hard in the SEAL community to remove stigma from PTSD. We now realize strengthening the mind to deal with unusual stress is just as important as strengthening the body. We do active outreach on the teams, but back then, it was not something you would discuss, even with your best friend. We might have shared a few anecdotes about being Vietnam vets, but we didn't go further than that.

George and I spent the day walking through the desert, recalling old times and catching each other up, taking frequent breaks, resting in the shade to talk. We were so close to the border there was no need to hurry now.

Buzz and I had begun the trip from Hyder, Alaska, on the 19th of June. George I hoped to finish the trip on November 19th. We had pushed it and now knew we would make it on that day. Now I just wanted to savor the time with George and enjoy the last few miles and moments. We put in about 20 miles that day, leaving us with about seven or eight miles left to get to the Mexican border.

We crashed that night in a rocky area beside the road. We were both tired, so we got a pretty good night's sleep in spite of the rocks.

November 19th was a momentous day. I could hardly believe we were only seven miles from the border. I woke up awfully happy, despite another night of heavy dew that left us cold and soaked. If anything, the condensation was even heavier than the night before.

Neither one of us could stop smiling. We split an orange and had a couple Lifesavers for breakfast. That got us back on the road. We soon passed the Organ Pipe Cactus National Park. We didn't take the time to stop because we were too close to our goal.

We then casually sauntered into Lukeville and had breakfast just a few feet away from Mexico. We had a good meal there in a place called Gringo Gap.

The day was all the more special because it was George's birthday. Every year since this day, I have called George to wish him a happy day and to thank him for getting me through SEAL training, Vietnam and the last 80 miles of my journey.

I was savoring those few moments before going over the border to Mexico and being able to do it with George. After breakfast, there was no point in delaying. We crossed the border and took a couple pictures. One of the pictures George took was of me next to a Mexican sign, "Alto," which means "Stop." Fair enough. That is where my hike did indeed stop. "The Hike" was done.

There was no way to express my feelings about finally finishing my long walk. I was far too happy to find the words to express myself, even to George. I was incredibly grateful to him for finishing it with me. Thank you so much, George!

Five months and, as nearly as I could figure, my hike encompassed nearly 4,000- miles.

Oh, these vast, calm, measureless mountain days, inciting at once to work and rest! Days in whose light everything seems equally divine, opening a thousand windows..... Nevermore, however weary, should one faint by the way who gains the blessings of one mountain day; whatever his fate, long life, short life, stormy or calm, he is rich forever.

John Muir
1862

CHAPTER 9
Taking My Next Steps

So many miles and so many steps, then my hike was over. With a big smile, I stepped back over the border into the United States and made the first few steps into the next phase of my life.

Those first steps were pretty mundane. We grabbed some orange juice and some cookies and walked across the road and started hitchhiking back to

Why. We did get a ride into that town, but we couldn't get one out. After being offered so many rides from Alaska to Mexico, it was funny to me that when I finally needed one, I couldn't get one.

We called George's wife, Maryleta, who came from Tucson to pick us up and drove us back to their ranch home in Tucson.

Dick Stauffacher, me and George Ganoung in Tucson after my hike.

Alaska-to-Mexico Hike Completed

By NEDRA BLOOM
Missoulian Staff Writer

'I suppose someday I'll take off again.' — Greg Burham, a Missoula resident who recently walked from Alaska to Mexico.

Learning from the mountains and getting to know people and lifestyles were the high points of Greg Burham's Alaska-to-Mexico hike.

Burham left Hyder, Alaska, June 19, and reached border town of Sonoyta, Mexico, Nov. 19.

A Missoula resident, Burham stopped in town in September for his brother's wedding.

Burham started out walking with Missoula high school teacher Buzz Blastic who accompanied him about 100 miles. And an Arizona resident, Dick Martin, walked about miles south from the Columbia Icefields with him.

But mostly, he walked alone.

"Most people aren't into walking — very far," he said. "It's time-consuming and most people have schedules and deadlines."

He said that when he walked out of Missoula he stopped every few hundred yards by wellwishers and friends. "It was like I was making the trip for all those people who didn't have the time," Burham said.

Burham said he hiked about 25 miles a day. "Traveling very slowly . . . you end up in a lot of strange places at night," he said, adding that he occasionally slept in ditches or culverts.

In Bountiful, Utah, he stopped at the police station information and they offered him a room for the night. It looked like rain, Burham said, so he decided to sleep in the jail. He was booked informally for vagrancy and went to bed.

During the night the shift changed, and when Burham awoke he was unable to get out of jail. He said it took about half an hour to straighten out the mixup.

Burham described himself as "a good deal fuzzier" when he set off on the trip, and he expected his beard might cause some troubles. But he said the police were very hospitable in most places. Several let him sleep in jail.

And no one bothered him about walking on the interstate highway, even in three states where it's illegal.

Other highlights of the trip were a rainstrom in the Grand Canyon with thunder echoing off the walls and a visit in Jerome, Ariz., a ghost town now populated with young persons who are "into crafts and simple living."

Burham also enjoyed talking with long-time residents about the history of their areas. He said he particularly enjoyed Utah and learning the history of Mormonism.

Before he hikes again, he says he has to "heal up." Pavement is especially hard on feet and ankles, he said. "You can condition muscles, but not joints."

He'll be going back to work as assistant manager of the Sparta Health Spa, the job he held before making the trip. But "I suppose someday I'll take off again."

I was disappointed that the Missoulian *reporter left out the fact that I finished the hike with fellow SEAL and swim buddy George Ganoung!*

I began unpacking and figuring out what to keep and remembered that from Alaska to Mexico, I found $2.80 worth of change next to the roads and trails. I wondered how much that meant I earned per hour during my five-month walk.

I was extremely lucky to be able to stay with the Ganoungs and rest for a few weeks, before flying back home to Montana. During my first week in Tucson, one of the guys whom George and I went through UDT Basic Training with, Dick Stauffacher, came down to visit us from his home in Denver. We talked about our future plans, with me hoping to finish my degree. We were all avid skiers and talked about that, too.

On my flight back to Missoula, I had a layover in Salt Lake City, so I called Craig Hansell, the Vietnam veteran sports journalist who had written the article for the *Salt Lake Tribune*. I filled him in on the rest of my trip before making my connecting flight.

My mother picked me up at the airport and we were so happy to see each other again. I moved back home with her. Fortunately, Doug Bitney rehired me to continue being a fitness instructor at the Sparta Health Spa. I called the *Missoulian* as they asked so they could write a follow up article.

My younger brother Kevin had finished his B.A. Degree in Sociology with a Criminology focus by then. That was the same degree I was working on before I set off on my hike. He was then doing volunteer work at the local Youth Court Probation Office, and soon after that he received a full- time job as a Deputy Youth Court Probation Officer

The Salt Lake Tribune *reporter Craig Hansell took a picture of all the gear I carried from Alaska to Mexico.*

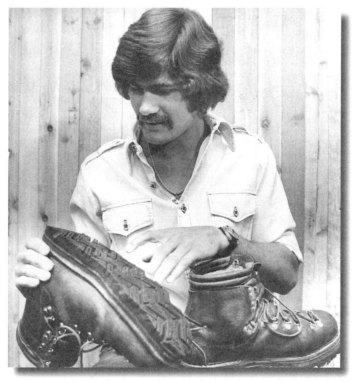

Tire treads worked great for my boot soles. Photos courtesy Craig Hansell.

in Kalispell, Montana, where he and I grew up. He and his wife, Jeannie, loved it there.

I had decided on my walk that I wanted to finish my degree and enter the field of counselling. I was about a quarter-and-a-half away from finishing my bachelor degree at University of Montana, so in a sense, I was well on my way. I supposed I could have enrolled in the winter semester. I did know exactly what kind of counselling I wanted to do. I knew I wanted to help people going through high-stress situations, but beyond that, I was still a little vague.

As I was sifting through my options, I received a phone call from Dick Stauffacher, the SEAL buddy who came down to Tucson from Denver to visit George, Maryleta, and I. Dick was going to college in Denver at the time and working the Number 3 Lift bar and restaurant in Denver with another SEAL buddy Bob Kirkwood, who was then a bartender and manager. Dick had told Bob that I had just walked from Alaska to Mexico. Bob wanted to hire me at the Lift, and he had a place for me to live in Denver. He also told me that I could ski as often as I wanted to in Colorado.

While I had made a lot of emotional progress on my walk, I wasn't quite ready to jump into the rest of my life and a serious job. Dick's invitation was so wonderful that I didn't re-enroll in the University of Montana. In April of 1975, I took off for Denver in a used car that I was able to buy. I stopped in Salt Lake City and spent a night with the *Salt Lake Tribune* journalist Craig Hansell.

When I got to Denver, Dick showed me around and set me up the nice house he was renting with a room for me.

Soon after I got there, I began my job checking IDs at the front door of The Lift Bar along with Dick. I soon graduated to backup bartender for Neil Langland. He was a great bartender and taught me how to be a good bartender, too. Between shifts, some of us coworkers exercised and played basketball together at a local health club. When the three of us were not working, we were skiing and living it up. It was great living and working with my SEAL Teammates. It was as nurturing a place very nearly as being on the Teams.

That summer I met and got to know Leslie Young who was working as a waitress in The Lift's restaurant. That fall, she returned to nursing school at the University of Oklahoma. Some months before graduation, she dropped out and came back to stay with her family in Littleton, Colorado. Soon after her return, she came back to work at The Lift. Our friendship was enhanced as we continued to work together and frequently went to breakfast early in the morning with our coworkers after our bar and restaurant shifts were over. That Halloween after our incredible shifts, the entire Lift crew went to breakfast, and Leslie and I ended up considering that our first date.

After dating and skiing for three months, we decided to get married on March 6 of the next year, 1976. I loved her and her entire family so much. None of them considered me a "crazy Vietnam veteran." Her father, Bob, was an Army veteran between World War II and Korea and knew about the UDT-SEAL Teams. He was an outdoorsy guy who skied, hiked, fished and hunted, so we had a lot in common. He was a volunteer rescuer for anyone who got lost in the woods. He did all that while he was a geologist for Mobil Oil Company. He understood and

The beautiful and kind Leslie Young became my bride on March 6, 1976.

was impressed by my walk from Alaska to Mexico.

Our wedding took place at the Evergreen Lutheran Church just outside of Denver. My mother, brother Kevin, who was my best man, and Aunt Agnes Lorentzen came down from Montana to attend. My uncle Daryl and aunt Ella Burham came over from Washington, Iowa. Leslie's entire family, her parents, Bob and Laura, her younger sister, Teresa, who was her maid of honor, and her brother, Tom, not only came to our wedding, but also they hosted our reception at their house in Littleton, Colorado. Our single-night honeymoon was at the Brown Hotel in downtown Denver. The next day we both went back to work.

I was very glad that Leslie really liked Missoula, Montana after we went

up there to visit my family while we were dating. I always planned to return home. A few months after getting married, we moved there.

I was ready now to begin my life. I re-enrolled at The University of Montana, and Leslie went to work at Western Montana Medical Clinic. Kevin introduced me to Jerry Johnson, the Chief Youth Court Probation Officer in Missoula, and I began doing volunteer work there while I was finishing my Bachelor of Arts Degree in Sociology, with a Criminology focus. I realized helping kids in the criminal system was my calling. These kids, for the most part, were dealing with serious trauma that was not of their creating and that was beyond their control. I saw parallels with

my Vietnam experience. When I finished my bachelors, I went for my graduate degree.

Leslie transferred all of her credits from the University of Oklahoma's Nursing School and returned to the University of Montana to finish her degree in education, with a focus on health and human services. As a result, we were able to live affordably in the university's married student housing.

After Leslie and I moved to Missoula, our summer vacations were car trips to Denver to spend time with her family and visit our friends with whom we had worked at The Lift. During the summer of 1979, Leslie decided to ride her bicycle all the way to Denver with a friend of hers. Knowing how important

Leslie, me, my mom, Jeannie and Kevin.

171

my hike was to me, I was supportive of Leslie's trek. Two–and-a-half weeks after they left Missoula, they rode into Denver after an impressive thousand-mile ride. I was very proud of her completing such a long trip under her own power.

In late 1979, after Leslie finished her education degree and student teaching, she became pregnant. On July 19, 1980, she gave birth to twins. The doctor didn't realize she had twins until after Jon was born. Thirty minutes later, Anna was born, too. They were each less than five pounds, but thank God they were both very healthy.

I was busy with work, the twins, and finishing my graduate degree in counseling. We both were very glad to have each other and two wonderful kids. Even as happy as we were, we were both sleep-deprived for their first two years. Fortunately, my mother did a great job helping us take care of the twins, especially the older they became.

On July 1, 1984, Leslie gave birth to Jacob. We then felt very lucky to have those great healthy kids. After Jake was born, one of the things that came to mind for Leslie and me was the talks we had while we were skiing after we decided to get married. Because both of us were taught to ski when we were six years old, we were very committed to being able to ski as a family by teaching our young kids to ski just as we had been taught. They all learned how to ride their bicycles early, too—Jon was six, Anna was seven, and Jacob was only four. They all loved learning how to swim, as well. Jon also became a very good soccer player in grade school. I enjoyed participating in physical and athletic activities during my childhood, as did Leslie, and we had fun passing that on to our kids.

Leslie's family, L-R: Brother Tom, Leslie, sister Theresa, mother Laura and father Robert.

CHAPTER 10
Teach without Teaching

"Training is never over." Chief Byers' words from my SEAL graduation echoed in my mind.

Despite becoming a SEAL, serving honorably through combat in Vietnam and walking more than 4,000 from Alaska to Mexico, I still had not really begun my journey and I still was not really prepared. I was about to receive some serious training. First there was my formal schooling.

Early in 1977, I finished my Bachelor of Arts Degree and was fortunately hired soon after that to manage the Youth Court's Foster Care Program. At night, I began taking graduate school classes.

I got another kind of education around the same time. I was always interested in spirituality and took a class in Native American Studies classes from Gary Kimbal, a professor who had served in Vietnam with the U.S. Army. Learning of my keen interest, Gary connected me with Jonny Arlee, the owner and manager of the Native American Sweat Lodge in Arlee, Montana. Because the Native Americans are a warrior society, he would hold sweat lodges, which were healing, cleansing ceremonies for combat veterans. He invited me to attend one.

Native Americans discovered Post Traumatic Stress Disorder treatment long before we did. The ancient sweat lodge concept fits very well with the current best practices for treating PTSD issues.

The sweat lodge ceremony consisted of a talking circle. Warriors talked about combat and they encouraged me to share things that I had never told anybody. That was the first time I truly felt healing occurring. They talked about spiritually connecting with parts of land and I realized I was spiritually connecting with the mountains.

The sweat lodge experience really put into perspective the healing nature of my walk from Alaska to Mexico. When I returned, I told Gary about my spiritual experience in the Canadian Rocky Mountains near Gita Creek. When I mentioned the "teach without teaching" part, he told me that I had had a "vision." My response was that I didn't realize that white guys were capable of having visions. We laughed, but I knew I had a calling.

In the fall of 1978, Leslie and I bought a house in Missoula. Fortunately, it was only about a mile away from my office in the courthouse, so I could walk to and from work every day. Since my Alaska to Mexico hike, walking remained a form of meditation for me. I loved it. Even in the winter when the temperature was below zero and there was ice on the sidewalk, I enjoyed it. Once in a while in the summer, I rode my bicycle to work. It was fun, but not a form of meditation, so I didn't do it very often.

Around this same time, studies of Vietnam vets were culminating into some real understanding of what made us "crazy." Back in World War II, they called it being shell-shocked. With a large number of study subjects and years of tracking, however, we were finally making progress. In 1980, the American Psychiatric Association officially recognized Post Traumatic Stress Disorder. Exposed to these findings and the diagnosis in my graduate school studies, I had an "aha" moment of recognition.

Still, a diagnosis only gets you so far. While I had a label now for what was going on with me, I had no good idea of how to deal with it. As much as I loved Leslie and the twins and appreciated the folks I was working for and with, my sleep deprivation was complicating my combat-related PTSD. I suffered regular combat-related nightmares. I was still very upset by how we Vietnam veterans were being treated nationally. Stereotypically, we were still assumed to be psychopaths and drug addicts. The villains in many TV shows and movies were still Vietnam veterans. I wasn't just upset with how these distortions impacted me personally. What truly got to me was to see my heroic friends on the SEAL Teams and the many other fine Vietnam vets I met be disparaged in this way. Having been there and having seen so much selflessness and bravery, and

Our family at Christmas 1984 – Me with the twins Anna and Jon, age 5 with Jacob, age 1 1/2 on Leslie's lap.

I didn't know that
Navy SEALS
got PTSD.

then coming home to watch these people vilified was hard to take.

Because I didn't know how to deal with what was going on with me, I feared that, given certain circumstances when I was very stressed out, I might injure Leslie or the kids. I secretly planned how I would kill myself before hurting any of my family members.

After wrangling with my fears internally for some time, I realized that I needed to get some clinical therapy. Unfortunately, I couldn't afford it. Then, in 1982, because my nightmares were all war-related, I consulted with Veterans Affairs. They had a contract with a local psychiatrist who gave me a psychological test. After the test, the VA treated me poorly and denied my requests for any help.

Luckily, my graduate work and my work with the Youth Court put help in the middle of my path. I met Dr. Michael Marks and Dr. Bob Shea, a Vietnam combat veteran, both of whom were PhD Clinical Psychologists who were pioneers in understanding and treating combat-related PTSD. I also met Phil Burgess, M.A., another Vietnam combat veteran who was counseling other veterans at the University of Montana. I continued to wrestle with the VA. Michael received a contract with the VA when I finally got benefits, so I began to work with him as my therapist.

I was drinking fairly frequently, but I wasn't really into the hard stuff, mostly beer. It wasn't a huge amount, but every damned beer I drank, it seemed to screw up my connection with my emotional life. My drinking didn't create major problems within my marriage so much as it created emotional problems for me. I was having difficulty relating to those emotions and sharing them with Dr. Michael Marks. With his help I began to understand and cope with my PTSD. I was in therapy with Michael, and also going to lunch with Bob Shea. Because the drinking was screwing me up, they suggested that it was time to quit. They didn't demand it, but counseled that it was driven by my PTSD. Michael helped me understand that the drinking was making the problem worse and preventing me from connecting clearly with my emotional issues. I quit drinking New Year's 1984, and I haven't had a drink since then.

I didn't know that Navy SEALS got PTSD. We could do countless pushups, swim miles in frigid water, and take any amount of abuse without quitting. Certainly we could withstand the stress of constant mortar attacks and heart-pounding ambushes. Getting blown up and shot is just part of our lives, isn't it? We should be tough enough to take all that in stride, I thought. I sure didn't want to tell anyone that it was bothering me and show that I was "weak."

With counselling, I came to learn that PTSD had nothing to do with weakness. Not recognizing and dealing with the stress was the weakness, not the stress itself. The strongest SEAL in the world will become weak if he doesn't recognize he is hungry and doesn't get food. The strongest SEAL in the world will become weak if he has PTSD and doesn't get help. I thought about the guys I served with and the guys serving now. Teach without teaching. I had learned something that was very important to share with my warrior brothers. I did not want one man to suffer as I had.

When I was no longer suicidal, I went back to graduate school. I began taking graduate counseling classes again with Bill Wilmot, PhD (an Interpersonal Communications Department professor) as my graduate advisor. Since I was working full time with two small children and a third one on the way (Jacob arrived on July 1, 1984), I was lucky Bill was so patient with me. I took graduate social work, psychology, Native American studies, and communication classes. Bob Deaton, PhD (a Social Work Professor) was another one of my graduate advisors. These men and the love of my family helped me complete my degree and get through the emotional challenges.

I joined a local group of veterans who supported Missoula getting a Vet Center. In the early 1980s, the only Vet Center in Montana was in Billings. We worked tirelessly and finally, with the help of Rep. Pat Williams, our Vet Center opened in Missoula in 1985.

Soon after our Vet Center opened, Phil Burgess, the University of Montana counsellor, became one of the combat trauma counselors there. I was active with local veterans' groups, determined to share my experiences and insights; teaching without teaching. At one of the meetings, Phil suggested that I become the group's chairman. In 1986, we were very lucky to get Richard Johnson, PhD (a former Vietnam veteran helicopter pilot) as our Team Leader.

In 1987, I finally finished my Master's Degree. I was glad to have done that because it made me feel like I was able to be a better Deputy Youth Court Probation Officer. Beyond combat, other situations that are common to sufferers PTSD are life in foster care and experience with domestic violence. The youth offenders I was counselling were no strangers to either. With my degree

and my own PTSD, I had a unique contribution to make towards helping these kids.

Later that year, Dr. Marks, my therapist, showed up with several copies of a script for a play he loved that he had seen in New York City. The play was called *Tracers,* and it was written by other Vietnam veterans. Dr. Marks wanted to do it in Missoula to raise money for some groups of veterans and educate the community about the Vietnam War and the combat veterans who had served there. He was the "Scooter" character and insisted that I be "Little John." We did it in the fall of 1987 and the fall of 1988. The entire play, including the background music, reminded me so much of several

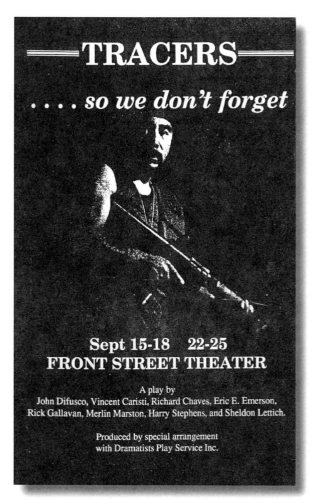

=TRACERS=

. . . . *so we don't forget*

Sept 15-18   22-25
FRONT STREET THEATER

A play by
John Difusco, Vincent Caristi, Richard Chaves, Eric E. Emerson, Rick Gallavan, Merlin Marston, Harry Stephens, and Sheldon Lettich.

Produced by special arrangement
with Dramatists Play Service Inc.

elements of my tour, so it was like doing therapy in public. All of the veterans who were in the play shared that they experienced that sense, too.

One month after we did *Tracers* in 1988, a group of us Vietnam veterans from all over the U.S. were invited to the Soviet Union by "Afghantsy," Soviet veterans of Afghanistan, to help them with their combat-related PTSD. Diana Glasgow of the Earthstewards Network in Seattle organized the trip. She spoke fluent Russian and was doing citizen diplomacy work with the Soviet Union during the Cold War. While she was in the Soviet Union in the mid-1980s, some Afghantsy pulled her aside and let her know that some of their fellow veterans were committing suicide, having trouble with alcohol and drugs, and experiencing other problems. They told her they had been reading about Vietnam and PTSD, so they wanted a group of us to come over and help them.

We landed in Moscow in November of 1988, one of three groups that were sent over. Our experiences were captured in several photos, newspaper articles, and a documentary titled *Brothers in Arms* that was aired on PBS (now seen from time to time on Turner Classic Movies http://www.tcm.com/tcmdb/title/456361/Brothers-in-Arms/). Our group had 20 combat veterans; five of us were from Missoula, Montana. Dr. Bob Shea was our PTSD expert, Roman Kuczer was our graphic artist, and Todd Brandoff, Steve Lohning, and I were the others. We spent our time there with the Afghantsy and their families in Moscow and Alma Ata, the capital of Kazakstan. They told us that the Soviet Union conscripted very heavily from the "Stans" to go to Afghanistan.

While we were in Alma Ata, we went to the local veterans' cemetery with the Afghantsy and the parents who had lost their sons in Afghanistan. They took us to their sons' graves and told us emotional stories about them. We connected very strongly with them, and

Roman Kuzar designed this pre-trip concert poster.

The veterans, interpreters and Diane Glasbow (top, center), who made the visit to the Soviet Union possible.

I ended up feeling like they were my family members.

While we were still in Alma Ata, the Afghantsy told us that the veterans of the Great Patriotic War, their title for World War II, wanted to meet with us at a small local theater. We and the Afghantsy sat in the audience seats as a half dozen of the Great Patriotic War veterans arrived and made their way up onto the stage. They all wore grey suits with combat medals hanging from their shoulders to their waists. Each of them gave a speech and they all thanked us very much for coming to the Soviet Union because we were the first Americans that they had permission to speak to since the war. With tears in their eyes they begged us to thank our fathers for helping them save their country when we got home. Then they asked us to come up on the stage, and they gave us all hugs and

The Cathedral of Vasily the Blessed, part of the Kremlin in Moscow.

I hugged one of the Afghansty at the memorial in Moscow.

Mary Ann Clark, our Russian language interpreter from Seattle.

kissed our cheeks. That connection was very emotional for all of us, including our American and Soviet translators. Since my World War II veteran father died long before this took place, I often share this story with every World War II veteran that I meet.

When we went back to Moscow, we were taken to their Afghan Veterans Memorial and a veterans hospital where we met a number of badly wounded veterans.

It was only years later, looking through photographs of the trip, that I remembered that we had a KGB agent with us the entire

Dr. Bob Shea and Roman Kuczer.

180

Snow storm at the Kremlin.

As important, respected, or admired guests, we were met with the traditional "Khleb da sol!" greeting of a loaf of bread with salt on an embroidered towel called a "rushnik." The gift signifies hospitality and long friendship.

Steve Lohning brought a bit of cowboy style to Moscow.

The Russian "Banja" is ritual community sauna bath that very much reminded me of the Native American sweat lodges.

King Harris, Jack Lyon and me back in Khazakstan.

Our group visited a graveyard in Alma Ata, Kazakstan to pay our respects to fallen soldiers.

I joined the Afghansty for a sing-along at a veterans hospital in Moscow.

Vladimir Putin, earlier in his career, was our KGB "babysitter," keeping watch on us the entire trip. He is sitting on the far left and I am in the center with the Afghansty at the hospital.

trip. That agent was Vladimir Putin! His career has certainly taken off since the days he acted as our babysitter.

the Vet Center. The people at the Vet Center had all heard about our trip the

Following that trip, in 1989 before the documentary was released, we had two groups of Afghantsy we met in Moscow and Alma Ata come to visit us in the U.S. Some of them came to Missoula. We took them to visit classes in grade schools, high schools, and the University of Montana, where men from our trip were teaching. We also had a great meeting with a group of local Vietnam veterans, including Jim Soular and the staff from

Jack Lyon, King Harris, and me (in the back) with the Brothers in Arms documentary staff.

184

Me with Bob Shea in Moscow.

The Afghan Veterans Memorial in Moscow.

Baikal Khamzin visted Montana and stayed in our home in Missoula.

year before and loved to connect with the Afghantsy.

My family and I were very lucky to have Baikal Khamzin stay at our house because he and I had made a strong connection in Alma Ata. Both groups were also invited to Native American veteran sweat lodges during their visits, along with the great translators we had in Missoula.

In the fall of 1998, the Mike Mansfield Center at the University of Montana (coordinated by its director, Phil West) to arrange a meeting of Vietnam veterans, both from America and Vietnam. They invited a number of Vietnam veteran authors and filmmakers to Missoula, including Jim Soular (author of *The Thousand-Yard Stare*) to meet with their Vietnamese counterparts. The Vietnamese were all former Viet Cong (VC) and North Vietnamese Army (NVA) veterans. I was very flattered and glad that they also invited some of us local Vietnam veterans who weren't authors or filmmakers.

Prior to our first dinner with the Vietnamese, I had read Bao Ninh's (a former NVA) book, *The Sorrow of War* and hoped to meet him. Several of us American Vietnam veterans arrived at the China Bowl Café in Missoula early and went upstairs where we were going to meet and have dinner with the Vietnamese. We were standing in a corner chatting as we waited for them, and I kept looking for Bao Ninh to arrive. Since I was a head taller than anyone in that group, it was easy for me to keep glancing around the room for him.

While Bob Shea, Jim Soular, Pete Lawrenson, and I were chatting, I looked at the top of the steps, and I saw Bao Ninh with a woman next to him, and he was pointing at me. I was amazed, so I headed over to him, and Pete followed me. The woman next to him was his friend Lady Borton, a Quaker lady who spoke both English and Vietnamese.

After the four of us connected, we found four table chairs in a corner, so we could have dinner together. Lady Borton told us that Bao just wanted to have dinner with other combat veterans. He would spend time with the professors and politicians later. She asked him how he was going to determine who the combat veterans were, and he said he would point them out for her, so I thanked him for pointing at me. He then thanked me for being the tallest guy in the group and the easiest combat veteran to find.

Logan Pass, Glacier National Park, June 18, 1998. Vietnamese/American Dialogue, Mansfield Center, University of Montana.
L-R: Le Van Thao (writer), Nguyen Ba Chung (interpreter), Pham Ngoc Canh (writer), Suh Ji-Moon (Korean professor), Ngyen Duc Mau (writer), Lady Borton (writer, Quaker Service), Bao Ninh (writer), Jim Soular (kneeling, writer), John Spores.

Bao, Pete Lawrenson (another Vietnam veteran who was then Missoula Chief of Police), and I made a strong connection at dinner thanks to Lady Borton, our translator. We discovered that Pete and Bao Ninh were both in combat in the Vietnam Central Highlands at the same time and here we were having dinner together in Missoula, Montana like old friends!

Before the Vietnamese veterans

Hanoi Vietnam
Bao Ninh

VIETNAM
014300ᵈ

To: Mr Greg Burham, MA
500 N. Higgins Avenue
Missoula MT 59802
USA

Never in a million years did I expect to get a Christmas card from a member of the North Vietnamese Army!

188

Bảo Ninh
317/3 Hoang Hoa Tham
Hanoi
Tel. 8471 433

e-mail:
baoninh@netnam.org.vn

Dear Greg Burham

Since coming back to Vietnam,
I've been always missing the
days in Missoula. I will never
forget good memories of the days
with you and with other American
friends, especially the veterans.
Please give my best regards
to them.
Merry Christmas
I wish you and your family
a happy new year
Yours

This inlaid plate was a gift to the Missoula veterans from the Vietnamese veterans.

left Montana and headed home, Jim Soular and John Spores, a University of Montana social work professor, took them all to Glacier National Park. Bao Ninh and I made a strong enough connection that I received a Christmas card from him from his home in Hanoi, Vietnam. I never thought I would live long enough to receive a Christmas card from Hanoi! Someday I would like to go back to Vietnam and visit Bao Ninh in Hanoi and go down to the Delta where my platoon served.

"Teach without teaching" became my life's work. When I wasn't counselling troubled youth, I was volunteering at various veteran organizations and other organizations that serve populations that deal with traumatic situations.

Since 1989, I had been a mental health volunteer on the local Critical Incident Stress Debriefing Team, founded

The Burham family gathered together in the fall of 2000 in Greenough Park in Missoula. L-R: Me, Anna, our great dog Gus, Leslie, Jon and Jacob.

by Bob Deaton, PhD. The CISD Team provided debriefings for emergency responders. Critical incidents were events so traumatic that they overwhelmed the normal adjustment responses of those firefighters, law enforcement officers, or other emergency responders who were involved. There were also unit peers on the team involved in the debriefings with those of us who were the mental health responders.

Richard Johnson, the wonderful Team Leader at the Vet Center, recruited me to be able to use my master's degree to help my fellow veterans with their combat-related PTSD. Within Veterans Affairs, the Vet Center program was known as Readjustment Counseling Service (RCS). Ever since I had joined the CISD Team, while I was working at the

Youth Court, the team members often discussed getting a Vet Center counselor to join the team, and now we did have one—me.

Not long after I got to the Vet Center, the VA made a national agreement with the Red Cross to provide volunteer disaster mental health counselors for major national disasters. I volunteered to do that in the mid-1990s. I was glad to be able to do it, and once I returned home after each disaster, I made a psychotherapy appointment with Thomas Clucas, PhD, a Licensed Clinical Psychologist who was a great trauma therapist. Every national disaster where I served would remind me of a sight, sound, smell, or something from Vietnam. As a healer, I myself still needed to do some healing. Working with Dr. Clucas helped me with the

My Red Cross dogtag inscribed: "Greg Burham RCS Response Team 9/11/01 NYC.

process of working through issues that my counselling was helping uncover. Training is never over and neither is the healing process.

The last national disaster I volunteered to serve was following 9/11 in 2001 in New York, where I worked closely with Dr. Alfonso Batres, also a Vietnam combat veteran, who was the chief officer in charge of the Vet Center program nationally.

I love the fact that through the Vet Center, I could connect with so many combat veterans and help them share things that they never told anybody before. I counseled World War II veterans, Korean War veterans, Vietnam veterans, and everything since. Then the Global War on Terror started, and I had a number of those veterans, men and

Buck Richardsom designed this "Medicine Wheel" pin for the Tribal Veterans Recruit Program.

women, coming back. I loved being in a safe place for them and facilitating the combat group programs. So many of the guys in the group said, "I'm hearing my story coming out of your mouth. I did not think anyone else was going through the shit that I did." About three-quarters of the guys in the group, when it was over, wanted to keep meeting weekly with other combat veterans, so I decided to continue holding informal group meetings. We called them "Here and Now" groups.

After I had been a counselor at the Missoula Vet Center for four years, early in 1998, Richard Johnson's doctors ganged up and convinced him to retire. As a helicopter pilot in Vietnam, he had barely survived two crashes. After he retired, I became the Team Leader.

In the late 1990s, Stew Brown, PhD (the Team Leader at the Boulder, Colorado Vet Center), and I were called on to go to the Bay Area in Florida to help some local Vet Center staff members deal with the sudden death of their regional manager. While we were there, we also attended a regional Vet Center staff training in Jacksonville.

At one of the meetings, Stew introduced me to Bernie Duven, a counselor at the Fort Lauderdale Vet Center. Bernie finished his Master of Social Work in Florida, lived in Colorado for a while, and was also a UDT-SEAL member during Vietnam. Because he had been in the West Coast Teams when I was in the East Coast Teams, our paths had never crossed. Connecting with a Teammate that you haven't met before is like being introduced to a brother you didn't know you had.

Even though we were counseling combat veterans on opposite sides of the country, we stayed in touch and became very close. Because he was in Florida, he was strongly connected to the National UDT-SEAL Museum in Fort Pierce, Florida. Fort Pierce was where the World War II frogmen were trained, so that is where the UDT-SEAL community put their museum. I had heard a lot about it, but had never attended one of their annual reunion gatherings, the Veterans Day Muster weekends in November. Bernie went to the Muster every year because he enjoyed being so close to the UDT-SEAL Museum. He suggested I attend when I could.

One of the missions of the National Vet Center program is outreach. Consequently, I had been attending the monthly Native American Warrior Society meetings on the Flathead Reservation in Pablo, Montana for several years, along with the powwows of the Blackfeet Nation in Browning, Montana. Because they were warrior cultures, they respected and honored all veterans. I loved doing that outreach and helping the Native American veterans get hooked up to the VA services that they had earned.

In 2001, Buck Richardson, a staff member in the Fort Harrison VA Hospital in Helena, Montana, James Floyd, a Native American who was the Director of the Salt Lake City VA Hospital, and I began the Tribal Veterans Recruit (TVR) Program. We recruited local tribal veterans to help us do outreach, so their fellow tribal veterans could get their VA services. I helped out with the three western Montana reservations: the Flathead, Blackfeet, and the Rocky Boy.

The following year, in 2002, our Vet Center team in Missoula (Dr. Nancy Errebo, a licensed clinical psychologist; Jake Stephens, LMSW and a Vietnam veteran; Jerri Skaggs, our office manager

and a Navy veteran; and I as the Team Leader) was found to be one of the Ten Best (of the 207) Vet Centers in the United States.

Later in 2002, my Teammate Bernie Duven asked the leaders of the National Navy UDT-SEAL Museum if they would like a VA/Vet Center booth set up at the next Muster. They said that it would be great. So I flew to Fort Pierce, Florida for Veteran's Day weekend to help Bernie with our booth at the Muster.

Jack Lynch, the then-President of the UDT-SEAL Association (we were in SEAL Team TWO together), came up to the booth, gave me a hug, and told me that he would like us to do this VA outreach booth at the East & West Coast Reunions next July and August in Little Creek,

THE WHITE HOUSE

WASHINGTON

July 1, 2002

Mr. Gregory Burham
Team Leader
Missoula Vet Center 0528
500 North Higgins Avenue
Missoula, Montana 59802

Dear Mr. Burham:

Congratulations to you and your team on being selected as a 2002 Vet
Center of Excellence by the Department of Veterans Affairs Readjustment
Counseling Service.

As we face the challenges of a new era, we look to our veterans for their
example of courage and sacrifice in defending freedom. The soldiers,
sailors, airmen, Marines, Coast Guardsmen, and Merchant Mariners who
served the United States made a lasting contribution to both the defense
and character of our country.

Our Nation owes its veterans a debt of gratitude that we can never fully
repay. This award recognizes you and your team's outstanding efforts in
supporting our veterans and their families. Your important work reflects
the American spirit.

Laura joins me in sending our best wishes.

Sincerely,

George W. Bush

Bernie Duveen (left) joined me at the UDT-SEAL Museum Muster in 2002, where I had the honor to introduce him to Rudy Bosch.

Virginia, and Coronado, California. We agreed to start that next summer.

At the Muster, I had the privilege of introducing Bernie Duven to Rudy Boesch. He was the Master at Arms in SEAL Team TWO when I got there. Rudy went through basic training during World War II, and ended up doing 45 years and 3 months on active duty in the Teams, making him the Senior Master Chief in the entire Navy for several years. In the Teams our most senior Teammate, whether enlisted or an officer, is honorably called the "Bull Frog". Rudy was Bull Frog longer than anyone. He also participated in the first TV program *Survivor* when he was 72 years old. He continues to be an extremely important member of the UDT-SEAL community, and he is still a member of the board of directors for the UDT-SEAL Association.

At the Muster, Bernie and I talked about our basic training and combat experiences. We recalled getting to the point of believing: "Even if getting killed in training is a threat, I am never going to quit." Unfortunately, that sometimes came true. Bernie told me about two guys in Class 42 on the West Coast who were killed free-diving in what was called the "surf zone," the location in training where obstacles were set up. They got tangled up in lanyards with the C4 socks and detonation cord and drowned. Jack Lynch told me that since World War II, when they started training frogmen, two men have been killed in training for every one killed in combat.

Bernie went through training class with Sen. Bob Kerry (Class 42) from Nebraska. Kerry was one of the three SEALs who were awarded the

One Teammate's Journey With PTSD
posttraumatic stress disorder

By Greg Burham, M.A.

By way of introduction, I went through training on Little Creek in1969 (Class 46E). After making two cruises with UDT-22 I transferred to SEAL Two in 1970 and completed one tour in Vietnam. I was only in the Teams for one hitch and didn't see a great deal of combat compared to many of those with whom I served. My heroes are my Teammates, past and present, who chose to make the Navy a career. Their expertise, courage, and commitment to the mission kept me alive.

I left active duty in 1972 and returned home to Montana to complete the college degree I began prior to enlistment. In hindsight, it was about six to nine months after leaving the security of the Teams that my emotional wheels started to wobble and my journey with post-traumatic stress disorder (PTSD) symptoms began. As I look back on the several months I spent in the Teams after Vietnam and before discharge I am very grateful for that time. While I experienced some nightmares, relationship problems, difficulty with anger, and was drinking more than I needed to, the support of my teammates was invaluable.

For the past ten years I have worked as a Veterans Affairs readjustment counselor and am currently the team leader at the Missoula Vet Center (in the VA we are known as Readjustment Counseling Service). I spend my working days with combat veterans from all branches of the military and all eras from WWII through Afghanistan and Iraq. It's a humbling job and one that I love dearly.

Every day I am thankful that I was fortunate enough to train and operate with the best. I have always maintained an enormous sense of pride in my association with the UDT-SEAL community but back in the 1970s and 1980s, on my own as just another "crazy Vietnam veteran," I began to believe there was something wrong with me. Miraculously, while living and working with a couple ex-Teammates in Denver, I met and married an unsuspecting local lovely in 1976. We moved back to Montana and by the early 1980s, she and I had three small children; I was working long hours as a juvenile probation officer and doing graduate work in the margins. At that time I was telling myself, "Stress doesn't bother me, I was a frogman for god's sake, I thrive on it!" Unfortunately, my internal reality didn't match up with that scouting report and the harder I tried to pretend that nothing was wrong the worse it got.

Mercifully, in all that confusion my friends and family helped me stop what I was doing and find a good counselor. I owe them my life. Asking for help was the toughest thing I've ever done and they made it easier by not shaming me into it. Today my wife and I have been married for over 28 years and the "kids" are in their twenties and doing well. Good timely help and a great wife made all the difference. The rest of my story isn't important except to mention that my approach to helping other veterans has evolved from the information and treatment approaches that I found to be useful.

I may be the only guy in the history of Naval Special Warfare who has ever needed counseling— the biggest weenie that ever made it into the Teams. At six feet five inches I have a running start at that title anyway. That's acceptable. What is not acceptable is having even one other teammate go through the kind of confusion and self-doubt I did, all by themselves. Several years ago one of my training classmates committed suicide in Chicago. His loss still brings tears to my eyes. For me the seed of this VA outreach to the Teams was planted then.

Prior to September 11th, 2001, less than one-third of the U.S. population could be expected to experience a traumatic event during their lifetime. Combat veterans have always been predominately represented in that group. However, it is worth emphasizing and reemphasizing that not everyone that is traumatized later experiences negative long-term effects or develops PTSD symptoms. Since the terrorist attacks, a great deal of information about this anxiety disorder has made its way into the popular press.

This article isn't meant to be a treatise on PTSD. My study of it dates back to graduate school in the late 1970s and early 80s, when I was trying to figure out why simply working harder and drinking more wasn't improving the quality of my life. I suspect that most of you have been exposed to information about stress reactions and some may know a lot more about it than I do.

As a long-time Association member I have never seen the topic addressed in The BLAST and would at least like to start a conversation about it. I understand that the politics of PTSD remain conflicted and confusing. As a result, I invite readers to filter this article through their experience and expertise and give me some feedback.

Much has been written about PTSD since it was formally recognized as a diagnosis in 1980 and was listed in the American Psychiatric Association's Diagnostic and Statistical Manual of Mental Disorders (DSM-III). In the early days a great deal of emphasis was placed on the traumatizing event when it came to predicting who might develop the disorder. The more horrific the experience the more likely it was that the exposed person would develop PTSD symptoms. Events generally thought to top the list were, and still are, surviving a life threatening experience, witnessing the serious injury or death of someone else (especially a person you care about), or taking a human life.

Given this list it's easy to see why combat ranks so high among stressful events. While a single discreet event may overwhelm some folks in a combat theater, all of these things may occur on a daily basis for a prolonged period of time. The current DSM- IV now suggests that the exposed individual's response to an event may be a better predictor. This would explain why two people can experience the same traumatic event and one is immobilized by it while the other remains unaffected.

We all bring different histories, strengths and vulnerabilities to a given situation, which is why I believe our training remains so long and difficult. We obviously want to weed out those who have difficulty handling stressful situations prior to combat. This brings up an interesting point about stress tolerance. Everyone who successfully completes training proves that they have an extremely high tolerance for stress. That coupled with the fact that we operate in teams and continue to provide invaluable ongoing social and operational support for one another, raises that threshold to an amazingly high level. And here, in my opinion, is the catch—it doesn't eliminate that threshold altogether. Just because a routine day in the life of an active duty SEAL involves a series of superhuman feats doesn't mean they (we) are no longer human beings.

I believe that we deny our humanity at our peril both as operators and healthy people. In my opinion, the warrior understands, manages, and even employs his emotional responses.

How to Score The Questionnaire on Next Page

24-32 PTSD is a clinical concern

33-36 Cutoff for a probable diagnosis of PTSD

37 + High enough to suppress your immune system functioning (even 10 years after impact event)

Measuring the impact of the Event

These questions are given to those attending a debriefing during the teaching phase of the PTSD treatment process. Below is a list of comments made by people after stressful life events. Please check each item, indicating now frequently these comments were true for you DURING THE PAST SEVEN DAYS.

	Never	Rarely	Sometimes	Often	Extremely Often
1. Any reminder brought back feelings about it	☐	☐	☐	☐	☐
2. I had trouble staying asleep	☐	☐	☐	☐	☐
3. Other things kept making me think about it.	☐	☐	☐	☐	☐
4. I felt irritable and angry	☐	☐	☐	☐	☐
5. I avoided letting myself get upset when I thought about it or was reminded of it	☐	☐	☐	☐	☐
6. I thought about it when I didn't mean to	☐	☐	☐	☐	☐
7. I felt as if it hadn't happened or wasn't real	☐	☐	☐	☐	☐
8. I stayed away from reminders of it	☐	☐	☐	☐	☐
9. Pictures about it popped into my mind	☐	☐	☐	☐	☐
10. I was jumpy and easily startled	☐	☐	☐	☐	☐
11. I tried not to think about it	☐	☐	☐	☐	☐
12. I was aware that I still had a lot of feelings about it, but I didn't deal with them	☐	☐	☐	☐	☐
13. My feelings about it were kind of numb	☐	☐	☐	☐	☐
14. I found myself acting or feeling like I was back at that time	☐	☐	☐	☐	☐
15. I had trouble falling asleep	☐	☐	☐	☐	☐
16. I had waves of strong feelings about it	☐	☐	☐	☐	☐
17. I tried to remove it from my memory	☐	☐	☐	☐	☐
18. I had trouble concentrating	☐	☐	☐	☐	☐
19. Reminders of it caused me to have physical reactions, such as sweating, trouble breathing, nausea, or a pounding heart	☐	☐	☐	☐	☐
20. I had dreams about it	☐	☐	☐	☐	☐
21. I felt watchful and on-guard	☐	☐	☐	☐	☐
22. I tried not to talk about it	☐	☐	☐	☐	☐
	___	___	___	___	___
Multiply your total by	1	2	3	4	5

Then total the numbers here: _____ = ____ ____ ____ ____ ____

He doesn't simply deny they exist. This can be a seductive short-term strategy because it seems like it works for a while. Alcohol may play a role in this denial/avoidance process, too. I personally ran this out as far as I could before I sought help. So what is it we're looking for following a traumatic event that can help avoid problems down the road?

Please keep in mind that we are talking about stress reactions here - not serious mental illness. Even the most extreme form of stress reaction, PTSD, is not about being crazy. It is considered a normal response to an abnormal situation. Crazy, as one of my professors used to say, is an abnormal response to a normal situation. PTSD is a treatable, and in many cases, preventable outcome of trauma. Good information is a valuable first step.

Jeffery Mitchell, Ph.D., considered the founder of the critical incident stress debriefing process, speaks of the "inoculation" effect of good information. "Forewarned is forearmed." Knowing ahead of time what the normal range of human responses might be can often help remove a great deal of the fear and self-doubt from the process. That can free folks up to deal with the reality of an event without all the added layers of negative self-judgment. I have been using the Mitchell model as a volunteer debriefer for the past 14 years with local emergency responders and in the wake of national disasters to include September 11th. In fact, this is the information and process, when properly applied, that I wish I would have had following my tour in Vietnam, or at least at discharge.

During the incident, or the event itself, well-trained people do their jobs and do them with precision. It's a conditioned response. For the reader who is interested in this process David Grossman's, *On Killing* is a great book. After a traumatic event or series of events it is helpful to begin to monitor oneself for symptoms of immediate or acute stress.

The bottom of the sheet contains another list of things to do and things to avoid if you are experiencing these reactions. This information, and the opportunity to discuss the event(s) in a safe confidential atmosphere, is the best PTSD prevention program I know. Should

CRITICAL INCIDENT STRESS REACTIONS

By: Nancy Rich, MA

Over the next month, you will experience normal reactions to the kind of experience you've had that may include:

Physical Reactions
Fatigue
Insomnia
Nightmares
Hyperactivity
Exhaustion
Startle Reactions
Health Problems (such as change in appetite, headaches, digestive problems)

Cognitive Reactions
Difficulty with concentration
Difficulty solving problems
Difficulty making decisions
Flashbacks
Memory disturbance
Isolating
Inability to attach importance to anything other than this incident

Emotional Reactions
Fear
Guilt
Emotional numbing
Over sensitivity
Anxiety
Depression
Feelings of helplessness
Amnesia for the event
Anger - which may manifest by: scapegoating, irritability, frustration with bureaucracy, violent fantasies

These are normal reactions, and although painful, are part of the healing process. There is not a lot anyone can do to make you not experience these uncomfortable feelings, but there are things you can do to feel more whole.

Things to try:

· WITHIN THE FIRST 24-48 hours, periods off with relaxation will alleviate some of the physical reactions.
· Structure your time - keep busy.
· You're normal and having normal reactions - don't label yourself crazy.
· Talk to people - talk is the most healing medicine.
· Be aware of numbing the pain with overdose of drugs or alcohol, you don't need to complicate this with a substance abuse problem.
· Reach out - people do care.
· Keep your lives as normal as possible.
· Spend time with others.
· Help your co-workers as much as possible by sharing feelings and checking out how they're doing.
· Give yourself permission to feel rotten and share your feelings with others.
· Keep a journal, write your, way through those sleepless hours.
· Do things that feel good to you.
· Realize those around you are under stress.
· The Nutritional Almanac recommends supplementing your diet with Vitamin C, B1, B2, calcium, and magnesium.
· Don't make any big life changes.
· Do make as many daily decisions as possible, which will give you a feeling of control over your life, i.e., if someone asks you what you want to eat – answer them even if you're not sure.

these reactions be ignored, denied or avoided in a variety of ways for six months or longer, they can grow up to be PTSD. Here are three PTSD Symptom Clusters:

- Re-experiencing the Event: Intrusive thoughts, dreams/ nightmares, flashbacks

- Avoidance Behaviors: Social isolation, emotional numbing, sense of alienation, "sense of a foreshortened future"

- Increased Arousal: Anger management problems, hyper vigilance, anxiety reactions, increased startle response, sleep disturbance, difficulty concentrating

The above may also result in clinical depression, thoughts of suicide, survival guilt, relationship difficulty, problems with authority, and a tendency to self-medicate.

Critical incident stress reactions are presented at the end of this article.

Fortunately, now I can look back and believe that all of it—the war and good therapy—made me a stronger person. Friedrich Nietzsche once said, "That which does not kill us makes us stronger." For many years that quote pissed me off. I now believe it's true, but I also believe that there is a lot of risky business in between surviving and becoming stronger. Talk and, at times, tears don't come easy to most of us—we are frogmen, for God's sake.

We in the Teams are a very special group of people and we have proven for generations that together we can literally accomplish anything. My hope is to focus a little of that "Hooyah" on taking care of one another in a way that we didn't when I was in the service. Again, none of this may apply to you. That's great. If you are doing well, please keep doing well. Perhaps some of this information can help with that. However, you may know a teammate who is struggling with alcohol or any of the symptoms listed below. There is help. Wherever you are in the country you are not far from a Vet Center. Please refer to the national phone list or contact Bernie Duven or myself at any time. Bernie

The Journal of Frogmen

Congressional Medal of Honor in Vietnam. He was wounded in action and had part of his leg blown off.

Every time we have a platoon reunion at a Muster, we also invite Keith LeBlanc, who was our Phoenix Program liaison, because, as he says, "spooks don't have reunions." We invite him because he lived with us and operated with us, did a great job, and was in every other way,

one of us. He was such a valued member of our SEAL platoon, that I recommended he become an associate member of the UDT-SEAL Association and the UDT-SEAL Museum Association.

Before the Muster was over, I phoned the Norfolk, Virginia, Vet Center and spoke to Lou Gunn, a counselor and therapist there, and he gave me the name and contact information for the best

Our family in Missoula's Pattee Canyon in 2005. L-R: Anna, Jacob, Leslie, me and Jon.

Veteran's Service Officer in the Tidewater Area to help our Teammates with their VA Disability Claims and get them better VA Medical Services.

I loved my work and fellow staff members at the Missoula Vet Center. It was great to be able to provide Readjustment Counseling Services for all combat veterans (from World War II, Korea, Vietnam, and all the wars after that), and sexual trauma victims. We were able to do this in a way that was not available to us after Vietnam. Once the Global War on Terror began in Afghanistan and Iraq, we were there to help waves of young men and women combat veterans. I was very glad to be there for them and our older combat veterans.

As a Team Leader, outreach provider, and a combat trauma counselor, my work went up to over 70 hours per week. That kind of work stress rekindled my own ongoing issues with PTSD. I still loved my work, who I was doing

Jack Lynch when he was Chief Petty Officer SEAL Team TWO. He was the President of the UDT-SEAL Association.

Bernie Duveen, Dick Stauffacher (who had come down to see me in Tucson at the end of my hike and who had gotten me the job in Denver where I met my wife Leslie) and I at the UDT-SEAL Reunion.

201

Lou Gunn and I at the 2009 East Coast Reunion on Little Creek after the business meeting.

it with, and who I was doing it for, so I didn't want to allow my symptoms to interfere. To help me continue, I began to see Dr. Tom Clucas on a weekly basis for my PTSD and Dr. Michael Hixon, MD, at the local VA Clinic, for my physical responses.

With our workload increasing, I got permission to hire a Global War on Terrorism veteran to help us with outreach. I was extremely lucky to have my friend Lt. Col. Eric Kettenring, M.A., an Iraq combat veteran; express an interest in the position while I took him to a welcome home lunch. Once he arrived, after some scheduled shoulder surgery, he not only did an excellent job with outreach, but because he had a Master's Degree in counseling, he was also able to help us treat those newly returning combat veterans.

Thanks to my coworkers (with our new office manager, Heather Kohut), my doctors, and my extremely supportive family members, I was able to continue this blessed work for several more years. My UDT-SEAL Teammate Bernie Duven and I continued to set up Vet Center/VA booths at the UDT-SEAL Association's East and West Coast Reunions and the UDT-SEAL Museum's Musters. Not too

Welcoming SEALs home from the War on Terror is a very important part of what I do. I want to do everything I can to make sure no SEAL today goes through what we went through. We work hard to help these guys get the services they have earned.

The Welcome Home Sign Group: Top Row (L-R) Gordy Henson, Don Johnson, Russ Verbeke and I. Bottom Row (L-R) Lane Cowart, Codye Jumping Wolf (kneeling) Ron Scharfe, Clarence Stern and Bruce Johnson.

The ladies honored Bernie, Lous and I for speaking at the Women's Breakfast at the East Coast SEAL Reunion.

Department of Veterans Affairs
Readjustment Counseling Service (15)
Central Office
810 Vermont Avenue, NW
Washington, DC 20420

May 26, 2009

Missoula Vet Center
500 North Higgins Avenue
Suite 202
Missoula, Montana 59802

Dear Fellow Veterans,

I want to take this opportunity to thank all of you at the Missoula Montana Vet Center for your strong commitment in assisting fellow veterans and their families. The "Welcome Home" signs you produced are currently hanging at each Vet Center nation-wide and here in the Vet Center National Office in Washington DC.

I have received so many comments from veterans regarding the message we project via your signs. One Operation Iraqi Freedom combat veteran related in Congressional testimony how touched he was when first coming to the Vet Center. He said that the sign you produced conveyed a message that every combat veteran appreciates, "Welcome Home." Greg Burham is a personal friend and mentor who has gone above and beyond for our country. First he served as a Navy Seal in Vietnam, and then continued to serve veterans via working for veterans as the team leader in Missoula.

I want to thank you personally for all that you have done, it has bought a lot of pride for the program nationally and promoted an essential Vet Center value, "Keeping the Promise." We thank and salute the entire team.

Alfonso R. Batres, Ph.D., M.S.S.W.
Chief Officer, Readjustment Counseling Service, 15

Vet Centers "Keeping the Promise" since 1979

204

many years later, the local Vet Centers took over the Fort Pierce Musters in November, and Bernie and I continued with the Little Creek and Coronado Reunions in July and August.

Jack Lynch continued to be the President of the UDT-SEAL Association. While we weren't deployed together, we both played on the UDT-SEAL football team during the fall of 1971. He was extremely supportive of Bernie and me and the outreach we were doing. In 2004, he asked me to write an article for *The Blast*, the Association's quarterly magazine, about combat-related PTSD.

Lou Gunn, a retired Navy Veteran and a great counselor at the Norfolk, Virginia Vet Center, was a Gold Star Father. Sadly, his son was killed on the *USS Cole*. Every year since 2003, he had helped us a lot at each East Coast SEAL Reunion.

Lane Cowart, a Marine Vietnam veteran, made a number of "Welcome Home" signs for the entry of the Vet Center. Since the Global War on Terrorism

was picking up, the group went into the "Welcome Home" sign business in a big way. Clarence Stern ended up making most of the several hundred red, white, and blue signs. The group sold enough of them to provide one for every Vet Center

in the country. Those simple words of gratitude and greeting mean more than you can ever know. Words can destroy and words can build.

Because I had a great deal of vacation and sick time built up, I took a two-week and a three-week break in 2007. Every day during my time off, I came into the Vet Center to catch up on my late written reports. I suppose the "as far as it takes, as long as it takes, whatever it takes" mentality of being a Navy SEAL was strong in me. It also covered up problems I was not dealing with very well. I suppose giving of myself so completely was a way of running from myself, too.

Not long after I returned to work from my "vacation," my clinical coworkers understood that I was having some trouble with my own combat-related PTSD. They knew that if I took time off again, I would probably still come in to write my reports. They recommended

Bernie and I were honored for our VA and Veterans Center outreach work over the years.

that I attend an inpatient PTSD program instead. My therapist, Dr. Tom Clucas agreed.

SEALs have a tradition of giving honest feedback and we also have the humility to take it. I called Dr. Michael

Missoulian

Guard changes at Vet Center

Longtime counselor to former soldiers retires

MICHAEL GALLACHER/Missoulian

"Every day has been a sort of gift. It was never work I did for someone. It was work we did together", says Greg Burham, who is retiring after 14 years at the Missoula Vet Center.

By MICHAEL MOORE
of the Missoulian

Greg Burham was a Navy SEAL during the Vietnam War. Burham, retired from his job as team leader at the Missoula Vet Center, where he worked for 14 years.

And like many soldiers, Greg Burham came home to a country that not only had grown to hate the war, but had, wrongly, come to blame soldiers for its existence.

Bewildered and unable to come to terms with his experience - "Who could I tell who would possibly understand?" - he decided to walk from Alaska to Mexico.

"What I needed to do was restore my faith in humanity, and that's exactly what happened," he said. "I found people who took me for who I was, and found a goodness that I wasn't sure existed anymore."

When he finally came back home, he found a job in the Youth Court system. There he heard stories from kids whose lives were infinitely worse than his own.

"I met kids whose journey through life made my time in Vietnam look like a cakewalk," he said. "It really gave me some perspective, and it also taught me how not to be judgmental. They were just kids in tough situations."

Just like Burham had been when he went off to war.

More than 30 years later, a tear still comes to Burham's eyes when he talks about his work at Youth Court and the Vet Center. A trained counselor, he's listened as both children and grown-ups have spoken of unspeakable horrors. He's seen them face those nightmares, only to retreat again to darkness. But he's also seen them move beyond the psychological plague foisted upon them by war.

"I've never felt, no matter what I've heard, that those stories were a burden," he said. "Every day has been rich in learning how the world works. Every day has been a sort of gift. It's never work I did for someone. It was work we did together."

Along the way, Burham found himself healing.

"Like everybody else, I was pretty much cut loose by the people who thought the war was a good idea." he said. "They left us on our own, and we had to find the way. The people I've had the pleasure to work with, well, they helped me find my own way."

The whole Vet Center concept came out of the dismal response America gave to returning Vietnam veterans. Missoula's Vet Center opened in the mid-1980s, and now serves hundreds of vets at any given time.

"What we needed was a safe place to go, a place where people wouldn't judge and would be willing to hear your story," said Burham, who will be replaced by Eric Kettenring. "Most veterans just stay quiet about their experience."

Burham said that people who've been traumatized - sexually, violently, in war or in regular life - need a place where they talk.

"If you can't find a safe place, you begin to think that you deserve whatever happened to you," he said. "That negativity builds, and it's a killer."

Finding someone to confide in is, quite literally, a lifesaver. Burham is honored to have been that person, for children accused of crimes and veterans trying to come to terms with the things they'd seen and done.

"I've been really lucky to live in a culture of talkers and make a living listening," he said. "I've always been fascinated with how people put their worlds together to make them work, and I've been blessed and fortunate to translate that into a life's work."

On Thursday, Burham stepped away. More than 100 people filled a room in the University Center at the University of Montana. He'd imagined his retirement might be held in a broom closet, so the crowd was a bit overwhelming.

The Veterans Warrior Society from the Flathead Nation drummed and sang, and Burham was awarded the tribes' medal of valor.

His colleagues spoke in glowing terms of his work, his compassion, his decency.

Then he spoke back, in words that reflected a man who is always giving back.

"Everybody in this room, in some powerful way, has touched my life," he said. "You've all given me so much, I can never be thankful enough."

Reporter Michael Moore can be reached at 523-5252 or at mmoore@missoulian.com

OPINION

Letters

■ *Greg Burham*

Article excellent portrayal of man

Michael Moore's excellent story about Greg Burham (Dec. 7) left me with a lot of different feelings, but mostly with a gut full of just plain proud. Proud to have known Burham for many years, proud to have witnessed so much of what he has done for veterans, and proud to see that Burham has been shown the acknowledgment he has long deserved.

Burham is, to those who have worked with him, something of a "gentle giant." From him I learned the healing power of a hug; to be given a Burham hug is to stay hugged. Through him, I and many others received validation for our various efforts during times of self-doubt.

Burham is a self-effacing man, and Moore's story captured that aspect of his character. But beneath his gentleness, Burham always carried a passion for the work that he did, and for causes that reflected that type of work. While calmly counseling those affected by war, he argued passionately against the policies that sent America's sons and daughters to war to kill other people's sons and daughters. Even those taking issue with his opinions respected the innate sense of decency that shone out from the man.

Burham credits those he worked with for whatever good may have come from their exchange, but that's not necessarily true. Others did their part but, in truth, it was Burham.

Burham is retired, but he will still be in Missoula, and I have no doubt that he will still bring hope and healing to a lot of people, including a lot of veterans. As with so many he cared for, Burham's wartime experience caused him to bear wounds that show no scars. But with so many friends, I am certain he will never have to bear them alone.

Dan Gallagher,
Missoula

Letters

ON A POSITIVE NOTE
Praise for VA health care

As an Army medic working ICU in a MASH unit in Vietnam, 1970, I came home with a great deal of "baggage;" most of which had to do with "survivor's guilt."

I had great difficulty getting into the Veterans Administration health care system, as the records of vets had been destroyed in a fire in St. Louis. With the help of Len Leiberger at the Army Reserve Center, my records were found on microfilm and I finally gained access to the VA health care system in 2004.

At the Missoula VA clinic, I was assigned as a patient to Dr. Jenny Murney, an extremely bright, caring physician; one of her first suggestions was to go see Greg Burham at the vet center on North Higgins. Burham turned out to be an old friend I grew up with in Kalispell. He was also a "Viet Vet" and a former Navy SEAL. Through counseling, he helped me understand "survivor's guilt" and how to deal with it constructively.

I have nothing but praise now for VA health care and the excellent care I have received from Murney and the entire staff at the Palmer clinic and at Fort Harrison.

My thanks also to Leiberger and Burham.

Peter Quande,
Missoula

UDT-SEAL ASSOCIATION, INC.
Naval Combat Demolition Units-Scouts & Raiders-OSS Maritime Units

P.O. Box 5965
Virginia Beach, VA 23471
(757) 318-3764
info@udtseal.org
www.udtseal.org

June 19, 2007

Dear Greg,

On behalf of the Officers, Board of Directors, UDT-SEAL Association membership, and the entire SEAL community, I would like to thank you for your 35 years of service to the UDT-SEAL Community, Department of Veterans Affairs, and to this great Nation for which you dedicated your life. Your unselfish contributions have provided a better tomorrow for so many, not only locally, but across this great Nation in more ways than you could imagine.

As a young Navy Frogman on a midnight recon swim or sneak attack somewhere in the oceans of this world, or as a Navy SEAL out for a midnight walk thru the jungles of South America or Vietnam, or a midnight freefall jump into a unknown part of the world, you were steadfast and always there for your swim buddy and teammate. As a VA Counselor you were relentless in your efforts to not only help local vets but taking your vacation time to come and provide those same services and information drastically needed within the silent UDT-SEAL brotherhood. You were continually there for your swim buddy or someone else's swim buddy, never giving in to the possible loss of a needy soul.

Greg, you are not only a tall man, but you are a giant when it comes to the seriousness of helping those who need help. You have given so much and expected so little. You labor over what is needed for those who are in need. You have taken the Navy Core values to a whole new level of Honor, Courage, and Commitment. You, my friend, are truly a SEAL for life. You have taken the SEAL promise of "No Man Left Behind" and in your own way have left no one in need without help!

We salute you, but most importantly, we wish you, Leslie and your family all the happiness life has to offer in your retirement.

God Bless,

Jack

Jack Lynch
President,
UDT-SEAL Association
Director, Naval Special Warfare Foundation
Director, Navy UDT-SEAL Museum

Congrats my friend

President: Jack Lynch
Executive Director: Mike Rush

UDT-SEAL ASSOCIATION, INC.
Naval Combat Demolition Units-Scouts & Raiders-OSS Maritime Units

Vice President: Gene Warta
Secretary/Treasurer: Heather Albritton

Chuck Williams and I at the East Coast UDT-SEAL Reunion on Little Creek.

Marks, my first therapist, who was then working for the VA hospital in Tucson, Arizona. He recommended that I come down to Tucson and go through their in-patient program, which I did that spring. It was a good program, for a bit less than a month. It was more than a little humbling to be a PTSD patient in a VA hospital instead of a counselor. By the end of the program, a number of doctors recommend that it was time for me to retire.

I made it back to Missoula before Memorial Day, so I had plenty of time to get ready to go to the SEAL Reunions in July and August. While I was on Little Creek, Virginia for the East Coast Reunion, Jack Lynch told me that even if I retired that year, he wanted Bernie and me to continue setting up our Vet Center/VA booths at both coasts with

me as a volunteer. I was glad to still be needed and wanted.

I did finally retire in December of 2007. After my retirement party, Eric Kettenring became the new Team Leader in Missoula. That year while I had time off, he had been the acting Team Leader and did a wonderful job.

Jack Lynch and I stayed in touch, and told me that the UDT-SEAL Association was going to start paying for my travel to the East and West Coast. He was very clear that he wanted me to continue the VA outreach for the UDT-SEAL community. Most of my Vietnam Teammates did over 20, 30, or 40 years on active duty in the Navy. Because I only did four years on active duty and one combat tour in Vietnam, I still feel honored to be of some humble assistance to members of my SEAL family.

UDT-SEAL Association, Inc.

CERTIFICATE OF AWARD

To

Mr. Greg R. Burham

On behalf of the of the UDT-SEAL Association and our members both active duty and retired, I would like to take present the UDT-SEAL Association Medal of Merit for your long standing support mentoring our members and the NSW Community on Veterans Affairs (VA). Your dedication in educating our community on VA benefits at the East and West Coast Reunions is greatly appreciated.

Our Association of former and retired SEALs, Special Warfare Combatant Crewmen and all the other personnel that make up the Naval Special Warfare Community greatly appreciate your time and efforts. Your generosity is sincerely appreciated.

Please accept this certificate as a small token of our appreciation for your efforts.

Dated: 19 July 2014

Chuck Williams
Chuck Williams
President
UDT-SEAL Association

National Association of U.S. Navy Frogman – Past and Present

After I retired, I continued to help on both coasts from the local Vet Centers. I will continue to do this as a volunteer for as long as the Association wants me to.

Sadly, in 2010, Jack Lynch died of a heart attack when he was only 66 years old.

Several years ago, a younger retired SEAL by the name of Mark Donald started a program called Members Life Assistance Program (MLAP). It is sponsored by the UDT-SEAL Association, and they help our Teammates and their families file VA disability claims and get better access to VA healthcare. They are doing excellent work for the entire SEAL community, and I will continue to help them, too, as a volunteer as long as they want me to.

I look back at this journey, through training and combat, the hike, and everything that followed with a profound sense of gratitude. The hike redefined me in every way. Instead of being a faceless a caricature of the "crazy Vietnam vet," I became that famous guy (at least in my home town) who had completed an epic walk. I went from being vilified to being admired, from being scorned to being supported. I went from not knowing what I should do next to having a clear life direction that has been deeply rewarding. Walking those miles brought me closer to my friends and gave me my beloved wife and family.

Today, I am honored to have earned the title "Vietnam veteran." To have been blessed to stand among my brothers on the SEAL Teams is something I thank God for every day.

Training Is Not Over.

-Chief Byers

CPSIA information can be obtained
at www.ICGtesting.com
Printed in the USA
LVRC02n2335041216
515034LV00013B/27

* 9 7 8 0 9 9 0 9 1 5 3 4 8 *